D1480487

RAPE WARFARE

The publication of this book was assisted by a bequest from Josiah H. Chase to honor his parents, Ellen Rankin Chase and Josiah Hook Chase, Minnesota territorial pioneers.

RAPE WARFARE

The Hidden Genocide in Bosnia-Herzegovina and Croatia

BEVERLY ALLEN

*For President Jimmy Carter,
one of my favorite builders,
with admiration and all
best wishes,*

Beverly Allen

New York

University of Minnesota Press
Minneapolis
London

April 3, 1996

Published by the University of Minnesota Press
111 Third Avenue South, Suite 290, Minneapolis, MN 55401-2520
Printed in the United States of America on acid-free paper

Library of Congress Cataloging-in-Publication Data

Allen, Beverly.
Rape warfare : the hidden genocide in Bosnia-Herzegovina and
Croatia / Beverly Allen.
p.   cm.
Includes bibliographical references and index.
ISBN 0-8166-2818-1 (acid-free paper)
1. Rape—Bosnia and Hercegovina.   2. Yugoslav War, 1991—
Atrocities.   3. Genocide—Bosnia and Hercegovina.   I. Title.
HV6569.B54A45   1996
364.1'532'0949742—dc20   95-25576

The University of Minnesota is an equal-opportunity educator and employer.

For Mimića

Genocidal rape: a military policy of rape for the purpose of genocide currently practiced in Bosnia-Herzegovina and Croatia by members of the Yugoslav Army, the Bosnian Serb forces, Serb militias in Croatia and Bosnia-Herzegovina, the irregular Serb forces known as Chetniks, and Serb civilians. Three main forms exist: (1) Chetniks or other Serb forces enter a Bosnian-Herzegovinian or Croatian village, take several women of varying ages from their homes, rape them in public view, and depart. The news of this atrocious event spreads rapidly throughout the village. Several days later, regular Bosnian Serb soldiers or Serb soldiers from the Yugoslav Army arrive and offer the now-terrified residents safe passage away from the village on the condition they never return. Most accept, leaving the village abandoned to the Serbs and thus furthering the genocidal plan of "ethnic cleansing"; (2) Bosnian-Herzegovinian and Croatian persons being held in Serb concentration camps are chosen at random to be raped, often as part of torture preceding death; (3) Serb, Bosnian Serb, and Croatian Serb soldiers, Bosnian Serb militias, and Chetniks arrest Bosnian-Herzegovinian and Croatian women, imprison them in a rape/death camp, and rape them systematically for extended periods of time. Such rapes are either part of torture preceding death or part of torture leading to forced pregnancy. Pregnant victims are raped consistently until such time as their pregnancies have progressed beyond the possibility of a safe abortion and are then released. In the first case, the death of the victim contributes to the genocidal goal; in the second, the birth of a child does, for the perpetrator—or the policy according to which he is acting—considers this child to be only Serb and to have none of the identity of the mother. All forms of genocidal rape constitute the crime of genocide as described in Article II of the 1948 United Nations Convention on the Prevention and Punishment of the Crime of Genocide.

Rape/death camps: buildings or other enclosures where Bosnian-Herzegovinian and Croatian girls and women are kept and systematically raped for weeks or months at a time. These are restaurants, hotels, hospitals, schools, factories, peacetime brothels, or other buildings; they are also animal stalls in barns, fenced-in pens, and arenas. Testimony indicates that more than thirty such rape/death camps are currently in use.

CONTENTS

x CONTENTS

INTRODUCTION

This all began for me in August 1992, when I got a phone call at my home in Palo Alto from M., a former student, saying she had something to show me.[1] M. and I had been friends for several years, ever since she had studied with me at Stanford. She is fluent in several languages and had been translating from her native Croatian that summer. What she showed me were her translations of dozens of testimonies of Croatian and Bosnian women who had survived two things I had never before imagined: *rape/death camps* and what we later came to recognize as *genocidal rape*.

The pages turned beneath my unbelieving eyes, pages and pages of the horrors of being locked in hotel rooms, schoolrooms, backrooms in restaurants for weeks and months on end, horrors of all sorts of torture and especially the constant, never-ending torture of rape. The women who had written these documents had made their way to refugee camps or crowded refugee apartments in Zagreb. Others had found themselves, finally, in refugee camps in Germany or Italy. Many others these pages told about had not survived, nor did all the survivors live past the abortions they attempted once they got away from the rape/death camps.

I was faced with a major cognitive problem: how to believe the unthinkable. The atrocities these women had suffered or witnessed were clearly the result of a combination of social causes: murderous misogyny coupled with rabid nationalism, all released by the specter of limitless power of one human over another, where the one with the power bears absolutely no responsibility, no accountability, for his actions. How could I accept this enough to believe it, when it meant the utter undoing of any social contract, of any basis for my own secure being in society? It didn't even offer the possibility of the misleading, jumbled reciprocity Hegel had found in slavery.

The voices of the women rang with the clarity of experience lived in the body, however, and thus they aided me past the impediments of my own hesitant, unwilling cognition. Thanks to their courage, my initial disbelief abandoned me to the greater horror of conviction as I read on and on. These documents were signed; several had photographs attached.[2] Whoever these women were, they were willing to be known, and, if what I was reading were true, this meant that their lives were still at risk. From that day on, I have been seeking answers to one burning question: what can I do about it? This essay is one response.

The first thing I did was to introduce M., over the phone, to a friend of mine in New York, Nina Bernstein, who is a journalist for *Newsday*. M. faxed some of this documentation to Nina, who in turn relayed it to her colleague, Roy Gutman, in Bosnia. Gutman's articles mentioning the rapes began to appear in U.S. media in early August 1992. Gutman has since won a Pulitzer Prize for his coverage of the war and the war crimes. Nina was sent two days later to Belgrade, to cover the Serb side of the war.

Since the U.S. presidential election was in full swing that summer, M. sent a packet of documentation of the mass rapes to Bill Clinton's foreign policy adviser. Shortly thereafter, Clinton announced that he was in favor of military intervention in Bosnia-Herzegovina. Once elected, however, President Clinton adopted a policy of nonintervention that has proven disastrous to human life in Bosnia-Herzegovina and Croatia, not to mention the aggressor Serbia itself, and has gravely threatened any remnants of moral authority the United States may have in the world.

M. next went to Zagreb to work with the Croatian feminist group, Kareta, which prior to the war had begun producing a literary journal. Now Kareta had become an organ of relief work of all sorts, with particular attention to the needs of women who had survived genocidal rape. Asja Armanda, a member of Kareta, has helped enormously to clarify the genocidal—and, as she puts it, femicidal—nature of these rapes.

Initially, the idea that Serbs could kill off the Bosnian-Herzegovinian and Croatian peoples by producing more of them, by fathering babies—that is, who would be half Bosnian-Herzegovinian and half Serb, or half Croatian and half Serb—seemed utterly ludicrous. The equation, more babies equals genocide, is a glaring example of faulty logic. I finally realized that, to its perpetrators, such an equation was possible on the condition that they cancel every aspect of the mother's identity—her national, "ethnic," religious, and even genetic identities—other than that as a sexual container. Later, I came to understand other aspects of genocidal rape. In 1992, I had not yet received much of the information that more recently has helped concerned persons separately and together to deepen our analyses. The Bassiouni database in Chicago was just being set up. But already, as 1992 drew to a close, it was possible to realize that the mass scale of the rapes and the other tortures, death, and pregnancy that accompanied them were aimed at destroying a specific social group, the non-Serb population of Bosnia-Herzegovina and Croatia, through the individual girls and women who had been and were being brutally victimized by this policy.

Very little news of this genocidal practice was making the U.S. media. I began speaking about it every time I had a public forum: in my classrooms at Syracuse University and at professional conferences, for example. Students in the International Law Society at Syracuse University Law School, under the initiative of Nancy Bell, a bright young law student in one of my graduate seminars in critical theory, organized a symposium on this outrage in April 1993 and invited M., Donna Ardzt, a specialist in human rights law at Syracuse University Law School, and me to speak. I began to write about what I knew. An op-ed piece of mine was distributed to newspapers throughout the United States by the *Progressive*'s distribution service out of Madison, Wisconsin. The Milan newspaper *Il Giorno* published an Italian version of that same article. The Italian parliamentary deputy Emma Bonino read it and invited me to New York to meet her at the Italian Mission to the United Nations. The Honorable Ms. Bonino knew about the rapes; she participates in an active lobby organized by the transnational campaign "No Peace Without Justice" to urge the United Nations Security Council to establish a permanent war crimes tribunal. At the time, she was heading a campaign to get a tribunal established to judge the war crimes being committed in Bosnia-Herzegovina and Croatia. I joined in this effort.

During the summer of 1993 I made contact with people in the United States and in Croatia who were working in war-relief efforts, both humanitarian aid and eventual legal redress, as well as people lobbying for European and U.S. intervention in the war or a less likely peaceful solution. Not everyone I met was willing to work with me; I didn't know enough yet, nor did I represent any institution. I began to understand that I was going to have to get much more information and then authorize myself. What astonished me during those summer months, which I spent in California at the Stanford Humanities Center, was that, in fact, some people in the United States, and many in Italy, did know something about the atrocities being committed. After all, there were people other than M.—Croatians and Bosnian-Herzegovinians, as well as people who still wanted to be considered "Yugoslav"—who were speaking about it. Gordana Crnković, a young woman from Zagreb who was finishing up her doctorate at Stanford that summer, had been speaking publicly about it for months. She told me how difficult it was to speak even to groups like the World Affairs Council in San Francisco. When she had finished her anguished report to them, their general response was, yes, all right, now let's hear the other side. The other side of genocide! The apparently democratic good intentions of Gordana's listeners had deafened them to the cries of the slaughtered.

Newspapers and the TV news on the western side of the Atlantic, at least, had almost no reports of the atrocities at all that summer. I was living in a kind of ambulatory anachronism, speaking about unimaginably horrible atrocities being committed even as I uttered the words to people whose lives were largely circumscribed by the immense physical beauty of the Stanford campus and the muffling cushioning it can sometimes provide as an interface with the rest of the world, even when that "rest" is as close as the drug ghettoes of East Palo Alto.

It was during the summer of 1993 that I began to hear that

videotapes of the rapes were sometimes being made and circulated on the international pornography market. I had no proof of this. One balmy evening, however, when I wandered over to campus to hear some Czech writers speak, I met a Stanford student who had just returned from a year studying in Egypt. We chatted about the things we were doing; I talked about my research on genocidal rape, and I mentioned that I had heard rumors about these videotapes. Oh yes, she said, she had some friends who had visited her in Egypt who had heard about these tapes somewhere in Eastern Europe.[3]

At the end of that summer I came to Italy for a research leave. From my autumn headquarters in the magical, lagoon-lapped beauty of Venice, I traveled to nearby Zagreb, where I met survivors, caregivers, and relief officials and saw for myself some of what was being done to help women like those whose testimonies I had read a year earlier. I also visited Karlovac, a city on the front line, where I saw for myself what being in a war is like. It was eerily like home for me. The landscape was like that of central New York, the October day was sunny and mild, and the bombed-out buildings reminded me of East Palo Alto or the Bronx. War, for all its specific and unspeakable horror in Bosnia-Herzegovina and Croatia, is perhaps no longer localizable only as international conflict. It is also, in other forms, part of the U.S. toposcape as much as it is the current reality in Karlovac.

Now I know survivors personally. I have spent hours and hours listening to whatever they want to tell me. I have met dozens of caregivers, from a young Canadian Croatian feminist who came to live in Zagreb at her own expense in order to work with Kareta to a Bosnian Muslim sociologist who, though she does not discuss it, is probably a survivor of genocidal rape, and certainly a survivor of a Serb concentration camp, who has lost her husband and her university professorship to Serb "ethnic cleansing." I have spoken at a conference about genocidal rape at the Senate building in Rome along with women from Bosnia-Herzegovina (some of whom are survivors themselves), Croatia, and Italy. I have learned the history of the war and heard testimonies from many Italian journalists who have been covering it since it began. I have been reading international law and have analyzed it with regard to this atrocious crime. I have spoken about it with the president of the United Nations International Criminal Tribunal for the former Yugoslavia, Professor Antonio Cassese, and with other experts in international and human rights law. I have organized an international conference in Zagreb, "Women, Culture, War," with participants, some of them survivors of genocidal rape, from Bosnia-Herzegovina and Croatia. I have written about genocidal rape in U.S. and Italian newspapers. I have been traveling all over Italy speaking about genocidal rape to groups, on television, and on the radio. I have done an interview on U.S. radio. Often, when I have a talk to give the following day, my sleep is filled with nightmares. Every time I meet another woman who has survived, or who is helping the survivors, or who is struggling to articulate the horror the survivors and the dead have suffered and to prevent its recurrence, my own anger and grave distress turn toward hope.

It is extremely difficult to write about these things. Every phrase risks misinterpretation; every analytic moment risks being incomplete. My own work is limited by my subject position, whence it simultaneously derives whatever authority it has. I offer it not because it is perfect but because I want things to change for the better, and this may help.

During these months, now years, of information gathering and analysis, discussion and processing, I have come to an understanding of genocidal rape in Bosnia-Herzegovina and Croatia that I articulate in six themes: identity, representation, facts, analysis, remedies, and implications. These give some form to my thoughts, even though what I am thinking about can never be bound by form, even though what I am thinking about is unthinkable.

Theme 1

IDENTITY

About Myself

I begin with my own identity, the aspects of this place called my self that made it ripe terrain for M.'s translations. Rape and other violence based on gender and sex are not unknown to me. For almost ten years, I have been working with groups of rape survivors and battered women and have come to an understanding of the psychological processes involved in recovering from such violence. This experience with some of misogyny's worst manifestations has prepared me somewhat for my relations with individual survivors and certainly made me more willing to believe the early Bosnian-Herzegovinian and Croatian testimonies than I might otherwise have been.

My engagement with feminism means that I try always to take into consideration the effects of gender and to work to undo and to prevent any and all injustices based on those effects. This does not mean that I hate men or adulate women as such. I see all people as liable to injustice based on gender effects, just as I see some people benefiting from them more than do others. The beneficiaries are not always men. Nor are men, even when they are the apparent beneficiaries, in a patriarchal system, for example, necessarily to be envied for their "benefits." Gender effects often require of people classed in gender-dominant roles behavior that is harmful to them and that may prevent them from much intimacy and pleasure they otherwise might enjoy. I have been able to pursue this work, therefore, on my good days, without always blaming the rapists as *men*. I blame them as individuals, as criminals, as vicious perpetrators of horrible crimes. And I also see them at the mercy of a sexist and nationalist ideology that forms them that way. The solution, therefore, is to cure the disease and, in the meanwhile, to stop the crimes and justly punish the criminals.

The third aspect of my subject position that comes to the fore in this work is my own perplexed unease with national identity as such. As the child of immigrants from Sweden to the United States, I felt very foreign, though I didn't know to call it that, as I negotiated the labyrinths of acculturation during my early years in school. My family lived in an insular Swedish community centered around the Swedish Covenant Church in Oakland, California. The big holidays were Swedish, and at times so were the preachers. The strangeness I felt at school led me to believe, therefore, that I was Swedish, not "American," and that I would finally feel at home only by going to Sweden.

I did that at the age of twenty, and thus experienced one of the gravest disillusionments of my life. Of course I wasn't Swedish; I didn't even speak the language very well. Nor did I act or think, apparently, as did the Swedes I got to know. Whatever we had as common culture was, on my part, years out of date. In Sweden, my Swedishness was quaint, a daily kitsch reminder of the anguished gulf immigration makes.

This identity situation got muddier when I began seriously to study Italian literature and culture. My acquired languages, instead of Swedish, were Italian, which I now speak fluently, French, Spanish, and, given the vicissitudes of my personal life, even a little Greek. I spent some formative years in Italy and have lived there for extended periods since then. In Italy, I am clearly a foreigner but less clearly, given my physiognomy, personal presentation, and accent, an "American." My son is a Jew, though I am not. Normalized patterns of identity are jumbled in me, although I am often encoded as WASP and benefit from all the attributes of being "white" in a "white"-dominant racist society.

None of this has cleared up with time. Instead, the constitutions of national identity that have left me feeling somewhat mid-Atlantic and identifying mostly with Italians, Swedes, and Jews in general and children of any immigrants in particular have become a focal point of my intellectual work and my professional activities. The person I am could not easily accept an explanation of the war in the Balkans based on blanket characterizations of *those* people as demonized nationalities; the person I am could not fail to note the role of national, religious, and "ethnic" identities, as well as gender, and of course politics, in the crimes this war has facilitated.

Finally, as a practicing scholar and university professor, I have the opportunity to pursue research in Italy, and at times in Venice, a city that constantly brings to mind the connecting power of the Adriatic, a city that is close, in fact, to Zagreb. The freedom provided by these occasional spaces in an academic's calendar that leave her free from teaching responsibilities for a while is essential to the sort of analysis I needed to pursue. It is also essential, I believe, to always improving teaching, which must have its base in my own intellectual and scholarly engagement.

M.

I now move on to the identities of the people who have educated me in this war and these crimes. M., my original source of information, is an American woman of Croatian heritage. I met M. in a survey course on Italian literature that I taught at Stanford in the 1980s. This course, based by departmental requirement on the national Italian literary canon, also contained my critique of that canon, and of canon formation in general. The sort of thinking we engaged in back then proved helpful to M.'s understanding of the gender dynamics of her own experience at Stanford, as she later told me. After graduation, M. went on scholarship to Croatia for a year in order to read feminist theory. While there, she got to know the Kareta group in Zagreb and helped produce the first issue of their Croatian feminist literary journal. After other studies in Europe and the United States, she is now settled back in the United States doing research in the law and working with survivors.

Survivors, Caregivers, Scholars, Journalists, and Others

Further information has come from many survivors with whom I have spoken in person on visits to Zagreb. I cannot name most of the women who have so generously educated me in this because to do so would place their lives again at risk, hinder their recovery, or further endanger the lives of women still being held in rape/death camps or concentration camps from which many of my informants have come. Their "ethnic" and religious identities include Bosnian-Herzegovinian and Croatian, Muslim and Catholic. Most of the women with whom I spoke were in their forties, as am I. Some are considerably younger, and one is in her early sixties. We spoke in English, Italian, or French, or, when necessary, with the aid of a translator.

Several women's groups in Zagreb have provided much of my secondhand information. This includes incidents that these women have witnessed themselves or heard of from friends or relatives. The Zagreb groups include Kareta, a group of Croatian feminists; Bišer, a group of Bosnian-Herzegovinian professional women, many from Sarajevo; Žene BiH (Bosnian-Herzegovinian woman), Bosnian-Herzegovinian professional women of Muslim and Orthodox Christian religions; Ruke, a Croatian group of women and men, many of whom are psychiatrists; and Bedem Ljubavi (wall of love), a group of Croatian women. I have received other invaluable help in more general research on the war from Nenad Popović, a noted Zagreb publisher who has founded a group to aid the families of journalists killed during the war, from Giuseppe Zaccaria, foreign correspondent for the Italian newspaper *La Stampa*, who generously placed at my disposal his own archives, and Adnan Kemura, one of the leaders of the Bosnian-Herzegovinian community in Rome, and his family. These people variously identify as Croatian, Bosnian-Herzegovinian, Catholic, Muslim, Jew, Orthodox, Italian, professional, working-class, men, women, city people, intellectuals, teenagers, doctors, farmers, refugees, displaced persons, feminists, survivors.

I am particularly gratified by the attention Professor Antonio Cassese, president of the United Nations International Criminal Tribunal for the former Yugoslavia, has given to my analysis of international law, and by the helpful conversations I have had with Mohamed Kreševljaković, former mayor of Sarajevo and now consul of Bosnia-Herzegovina in Italy. Other scholars of international law and human rights law such as Giandonato Caggiano and Sara Cavelli of the Italian Association of International Organizations in Rome, Rafaëlle Maison and Angela Ward of the European University Institute in Florence, and Maria Spinedi and Antonio Tanca of the Faculty of Jurisprudence at the University of Florence have been generous with their knowledge and their time. This text results from their interlocution as well as the testimony and conversation I found in Zagreb and Karlovac, Venice, Turin, Florence, Rome, Formia, Pescara, Syracuse, Trieste, New York, Palo Alto, and San Francisco; all its shortcomings are my own.

Religious or "Ethnic" Identities[1]

Now I come to the play of identities in the war itself. Observers in the United States often think of the war in the Balkans as the most recent in an endless series of violent conflicts that somehow characterize *those people*. Colleagues who should know better have told me that there's nothing *anyone* can do because *they* have been at each other's throats for centuries. The thicket of pronouns gets dark pretty fast in such talk. The *anyone* who "can't do anything" would of course be *us*, us non-Balkan persons. Yet even the most cursory glance at "our" histories would show similar serial bloodshed from, if we are U.S. persons, the American Revolution to the Gulf War or, if we are Europeans, from the Crusades and the Inquisition to the world wars, that no labels of "civilization" as opposed to "barbarism" can cover up. The demonization of the Balkan peoples happens to a somewhat lesser degree in Italy, where one or two generations still remember World War II and the ensuing civil war, when "Italian" atrocities occurred that haven't yet passed the line that hazily divides history from legend.

In bold opposition to the reductive attitudes I often encounter in the United States, my Bosnian-Herzegovinian and Croatian informants have often insisted that their national or "ethnic" identities, which over decades of national unity had taken on secondary status, assumed new values when the military violence began in 1991. A tolerant, multicultural attitude had characterized many of the cities of Yugoslavia in general, Bosnian cities in particular. People of Croatian, Bosnian-Herzegovinian, or Serb-Montenegrin culture, and of Catholic, Muslim, and Orthodox Christian religion, often intermarried without a second thought of "ethnic" or religious congruence. Their communitarian attitude came from other identities, what might be considered class-topographic ones, mostly as city dwellers or as farmers.

When the first shots were fired, however, people learned that their "ethnic" identity could now determine whether they were to live or to die. Although many people had felt mainly Croatian, Bosnian-Herzegovinian, or Serb-Montenegrin, those who had felt "Yugoslav" now became, many of them reluctantly, "Bosnians," "Croats," "Serbs," or "Muslims." This weapons-enforced identity slippage reminds me of my own distress when, in Berkeley during the late 1960s, the Black Panthers openly began arming themselves. The move to a potential armed conflict reinforced even the apparent "racial" differences between persons called "blacks" and "whites" at the time, and political affinities got swept under a rug of potential violence that now held only "race" in its weave.

The political basis for Serb aggression and Bosnian-Herzegovinian and Croatian resistance, and for Croatian aggression, must be kept in mind. Decades of dictatorship created sectors of privilege and oppression that now are being renegotiated by means of war and genocide. People who consider themselves "Yugoslav" may have been privileged under the regime, for example. People whose identities are nation-specific ("Croatian," say, or "Montenegrin") may not. This is no strict rule of thumb, however. Such political bases merit a study this book does not aim to provide.[2] They are all entwined, however with the "ethnic" identities I am concerned about here.

It is difficult for U.S. persons to imagine the workings of the racism in Bosnia-Herzegovina, Croatia, and Serbia because that racism is not based on the very thing U.S. people think constitutes "race": skin color.[3] How, then, do the people in the Balkans know whom to hate? How, then, do they know whom to shell, to rape, to butcher?

They know by other cultural markings: family names, first names, sometimes by towns of provenance. Of course such knowing depends on some sort of communication beyond simply the visual encodings that hold color-based racism in place. Often, however, this knowledge is based on assumption. There are also cases, moreover, in which "ethnic" identity is not a basis for enmity, as in the case of Sarajevo, where the Serb army has been shelling a mixed population that includes, in addition to Bosnian-Herzegovinian Muslims, Catholics, and Jews, also Bosnian-Herzegovinian Orthodox Christians—or Serbs—whose choice is to remain Sarajevan even at the risk of their lives.

Geopolitical Identities

The identity issues here are clearly matters of life and death. They are also a matter of nation-state legitimacy and eventual liability

at the International Court of Justice or at the United Nations International Criminal Tribunal for the former Yugoslavia. If, for
example, we insist, as do the Italian media, on calling the groups
at war "ex-Yugoslavia," we explicitly refuse to recognize the independent status of the nation-states Slovenia, Croatia, and Bosnia-
Herzegovina, as well as the reality of present-day Yugoslavia
(sometimes called rump Yugoslavia or Serbia-Montenegro). Although it implies that the war, which is a war of Serb aggression
against Croatia and Bosnia-Herzegovina (and which later also became a war of Croatian aggression against Bosnia-Herzegovina),
is actually a civil war, the "ex-Yugoslavia" term itself refers in the
end to a no-place, with no government, no inhabitants, no legal
status, and no identity other than as a cipher for the convenience
of those who haven't yet fully recognized all the terms of this
conflict.

Instead, we must take seriously the independent nation-state
status, recognized internationally since 1991, of Slovenia, Croatia,
and Bosnia-Herzegovina, and the resultant existence of the nation-state entity of Yugoslavia (Serbia-Montenegro). Not only will
this help to demystify the current war, it will have long-term effects on the proceedings of any international tribunal against war
criminals. International legal conventions or protocols can be
used to prosecute crimes committed internally to any given nation-state only in very specific situations. If, therefore, the media
or anyone else persists in calling the parties to the conflict "ex-
Yugoslavia" or the war of aggression a "civil war," such persons
may actually be working against the successful jurisdiction of the
International Court of Justice, which can prosecute states for war
crimes in international conflicts, and the United Nations International Criminal Tribunal, which is authorized by the signatory

nations to prosecute individuals for such crimes. For the sake of honest representation and fair jurisdiction, then, let us speak clearly about the nation-state identity of the parties to the conflict: Croatia, an internationally recognized independent nation-state since January 1992; Bosnia-Herzegovina, an internationally recognized independent nation-state since April 1992; Yugoslavia, the Serbia-Montenegro nation-state resulting from the secession of Slovenia (1991), Croatia, and Bosnia-Herzegovina from the federated republics that once formed the larger nation-state of Yugoslavia, which no longer exists.

These nation-states, along with the republic of Macedonia and the autonomous regions of Vojvodina and Kosovo, exist as social entities on territory where Illyrian peoples settled before the seventh century B.C.E.[4] These territories came under the rule of the Roman Empire, which by the fourth century C.E. had divided in two, with the border between the Western and Byzantine empires running right through the Balkans. This binary division, which bears all the differences of a mirroring, marks the simultaneous alienation and similarity that characterized the subsequent division of the Christian church into Roman and Orthodox rites and communities. Such rank paradox of likeness and difference continues to mark what we now call Western and Eastern Europe, whose conflicts are the sociocultural versions of the violence and upheaval that occur when two tectonic plates grate together to produce new geological formations. I must never forget that many of the aspects of the cultures that produce my own identities are determined by the historic events that produced and depended on this line of European identity difference called the Balkans. Even though it is not my life that is now at stake on the fault

line, it is clearly my cultural heritage that has produced and maintained the fault.

During the fifth and sixth centuries C.E., the Slav peoples entered these Illyrian territories, and Slav tribal communities eventually formed into the Bosnian, Croatian, Serb, Slovenian, Macedonian, and Montenegrin nations. As Weinberg and Wilsnack
note by way of clarifying the curious semiautonomous status of
several regions, the feudal system allowed several small social and
territorial entities to retain their independence. Dalmatia and
Slavonia were examples of this in Croatia, as were Herzegovina
in Bosnia and Kosovo and Vojvodina in Serbia (Weinberg and
Wilsnack, 1).

Another identity category that comes into play in these historical considerations is that of the Bogomils, a medieval Christian
sect that practiced tolerance and pacifism and that was considered
heretical by the Roman church. The Ottoman Turks, who came
into the Balkan territories in the fourteenth century, gained the
trust of the Bogomil peasants, who were in revolt against their
Catholic Hungarian oppressors, and annexed Bosnia to the Ottoman Empire. Over time, the Bogomils gradually converted to the
religion of their protectors, thus producing the peculiar European
version of Islam that characterizes the Bosnian Muslims.

I first learned of the Bogomil culture from a Sarajevo woman, a
sociologist friend whose name I will not say. During the six hours
she spent closeted in my Zagreb hotel room with me and our
translator one snowy day, and in spite of her almost constant tears
and grave distress, she insisted that the single most important
thing I must understand was, precisely, the history of the Bogomils. But the identity called "Bogomil" is irrevocably situated for

me within her telling of it, and so I insert here not any generic history, but her particular version of the history, of this significant, and for me previously quite invisible, identity. I quote her from my notes.

Europe and the United States have failed their humanity test. But Bosnia has a huge army, growing all the time. We will survive, even in reduced numbers. And we will remember everything. We have the impression that Europe is testing the limits of human suffering. Journalists declare this without shame. Our children look like old people.

Here are the differences in values and, consequently, careers, between Orthodox people (Serbs), Catholics (Croats), and Muslims in Bosnia. Orthodox people venerate the warrior, and therefore aggression. Their most important literature is epic poetry, that is, the literature of war and military prowess. Orthodox people choose careers in the juridical sciences and in the humanities, but they do not become scientists. Catholics attribute no value to the warrior. Instead, they greatly admire the priest as intercessor between human beings and God. They choose careers in technology. Likewise, Muslims attribute no value to the warrior. But, unlike the Catholics, they venerate the politician. This is the result of the decades of communism, when politicians counted most in society, while Muslim "priests" were neither very numerous nor very educated. Like the Catholics but unlike the Orthodox, Muslims tend to choose careers in technology. These statements are the results of a study done by a colleague at the University of Sarajevo.

Bosnia's army needs help. It has people of all these identities in it.

My husband, a Muslim engineer, was killed in Iraq in 1989. He was working in an airport and was killed during the Iran-Iraq war. He and the only other Muslim who had gone on this technical mission were killed in what the Serb authorities said was an automobile accident. But their car just blew up in the middle of the desert. My husband came from an aristocratic Muslim family. The Serbs killed him, even over there in Iraq. This was part of "ethnic cleansing" already.

We are the Bogomils, a name that means "dear to God." We have a particular mentality—we are against violence. Look at the history of the eleventh-century Bogomil Kulinbanis. Because of this Bogomil mentality of ours, heretics have always been welcome in Bosnia. Jews could always come, and they shall always be able to live in Bosnia-Herzegovina. When the Sephardim were banished from Spain, many came to Bosnia. The Inquisition wanted to do "ethnic cleansing" in Spain, but Sultan Bayazit opened our Bosnian territory to the Jews from Spain, the Sephardim. Sultan Bayazit told King Ferdinand that he was stupid to have so impoverished his own country in sending the Jews away. Up until the Second World War, there were something like twelve thousand Jews in Bosnia; since then there have been only about twelve hundred. The Sarajevan Jews offered their synagogue as an arms depot, thinking the Serb army wouldn't shell a religious building that wasn't a mosque. The Jews have given *everything* for Sarajevo and have been especially courageous. Now, Bosnia-Herzegovina offers the only oasis of hope of multicultural community for future peoples.

By 1992 the Yugoslav Army had already systematically "ethnically cleansed" itself of non-Serbs, even by sending young draftees home from boot camp in coffins. This had been going on for years. Nonetheless, when the army took up positions in the hills around Sarajevo, we Sarajevans still thought of it as the Yugoslav *National* Army or the Yugoslav *People's* Army. What treachery! It had already become a Serb army, but by the time we realized it, it was too late—the first Serb trenches had already been dug.

At one point, this Serb army went into family tombs in the Jewish cemetery, which is located on a hill so it can face Jerusalem. In these tombs, they actually built rudimentary elevators so that the soldiers would rise from the tombs, shoot in every direction, kill civilians, and then disappear back into the earth. They are still doing this; the cemetery is in a very strategic position.

My informant shows me a newspaper article from *Oslobodjenje* (Liberation), the Sarajevo newspaper that has been publishing throughout the siege. It quotes the president of the Jewish community of Sarajevo, Ivica Čerešnješ, as saying:

When the Serb soldiers went down into our cemetery, I gave permission to the Bosnia-Herzegovina Army to bomb the Jewish cemetery and thus destroy one of the Chetnik strongholds around Sarajevo. The degree of my personal and moral responsibility in this is clear, first to our Jewish community and then to the entire world. But I want to save the children and all the people.

The Bosnia-Herzegovina Army had not bombed the cemetery, however. Ivica adds: "We know who watches over and defends this cemetery; it's the Bosnia-Herzegovina Army. This we shall never forget."

We discuss this article for some time, and then my sociologist informant from Sarajevo continues her discussion of Bosnian-Herzegovinian identities:

Journalists shouldn't call the Bosnia-Herzegovina Army "Muslim." It is citizens defending their people, and the citizens of Bosnia are of many ethnicities. Stjepan Siber, who is one of the commanders of the Bosnia-Herzegovina Army, is a Bosnian Catholic. In an interview in *Slobodna Dalmacija* on January 24, 1993, he said, "We are *not* a Muslim army. Under our command the army consists of 18.3 percent Croats, and in some of our units we have up to 35 percent

Bosnian Serbs. Obviously the majority of our soldiers are Muslims, because 44.7 percent of the Bosnian population is Muslim."

Recognizing the identities present in the Bosnia-Herzegovina Army is a step toward understanding Bosnian-Herzegovinian society as a whole. My informant is not implying that the fewer Muslims there are, the better.

I step back into the chronological line here with the famous Battle of Kosovo, where in 1389 Serbia, loath to lose its independence, fell nonetheless to the Ottoman Turks. Present-day Serb nationalists hark back to this battle as the beginning of five centuries of Ottoman rule and the symbol par excellence of their right to take vengeance on all Muslims.

The Balkan territories in the sixteenth century were the terrain of the conflict between the Ottoman and Hapsburg empires. When the Austro-Hungarian Empire was formed, Vienna took control of Slovenia and Croatia, the more Catholic regions of the Balkans, while the Turks continued to rule in Bosnia, Serbia, and Macedonia, the Islamic and Orthodox regions. During this time much of the Serb population emigrated from Kosovo, which eventually became inhabited mostly by Albanian peoples (descendants of the pre-C.E. Illyrians) who had converted to Islam, thus establishing a regional cultural community that persists to the present day.

Kosovo, like Vukovar a formerly autonomous region within the Republic of Serbia, is now facing a terrible situation in which 80 percent of the population, who identify as Albanians, who speak Albanian, and whose religious identities are Muslim or Catholic, are severely oppressed by the Serb minority. This oppression is both in reaction to the Albanians' declaration of independence

(July 7, 1990) and in line with Belgrade's ongoing policy of "ethnic cleansing." In the case of Kosovo, such a policy would rid the region of its Albanian inhabitants in order to repopulate the area with Serbs from Croatia and Bosnia-Herzegovina.

I shall never forget when I was visited in Florence early in 1994 by Dr. Fatmir Sejdiu, a member of the clandestine but democratically elected Albanian Presidential Council. Sent to me by Muhamed Kreševljaković, former mayor of Sarajevo and present consul of Bosnia-Herzegovina in Italy, Dr. Sejdiu described the desperate situation of the Kosovan Albanians, who are persecuted in every possible way, from having their language effectively abolished and their schools outlawed to being routinely tortured and subjected to random atrocities. Dr. Sejdiu is a leader of the Kosovan Council for the Defense of Human Rights and Freedoms in Priština. He, along with the (clandestine Albanian) president of Kosovo, Ibrahim Rugova, are adamantly dedicated to nonviolent means of resolution, even in the midst of two cultures, the Albanian and the Serb, that advocate vengeance (Salvoldi and Gjergji; Council for the Defence of Human Rights and Freedoms in Priština).

With the advent of the French Revolution, creeds of both southern Slav (or *yugo-slav*) unity and regional nationalisms grew. In spite of violent Turkish repression, a semi-independent Serb state was established by 1830. Sultan Selim III recognized Montenegro's independence in 1899, while powerful clandestine groups agitated for Macedonian nationalism throughout the later part of the century. With Serb support, Bosnian Christians rebelled against the Ottomans. Austria annexed Bosnia in 1908, and in 1912 Serbia allied with Greece, Bulgaria, and Russia in the First Balkan War, which led to the defeat of the Turkish rulers. Shortly thereafter, the Second Balkan War began with Serbia, backed by Greece and Romania, challenging Bulgaria for control over Macedonia.

Serb nationalist fervor now began to regard the Austro-Hungarian Empire not as an ally against the Ottoman Turks but rather as yet another historical barrier to the realization of its legendary dream of the vastly extended territories of a "Great Serbia."[5] The Serb government began supporting the Black Hand, a clandestine Serb nationalist organization operating in Bosnia and Croatia, which were still part of the Hapsburg Empire. As Weinberg and Wilsnack note, the 1914 assassination in Sarajevo of Austro-Hungarian Archduke Ferdinand—the spark that ignited World War I—was likely committed by a Serb nationalist from the Black Hand.

Austria attacked Serbia, and the European nation-states chose sides. Russia, the United Kingdom, France, and eventually the United States lined up with Serbia, while Germany joined Vienna. Greece and Romania joined Serbia against Bulgaria and Turkey. When the Bolshevik Revolution began, Russia withdrew from the war. Finally, in 1918, both the Ottoman and the Austro-Hungarian empires, the last pre-nation-state strongholds of the division of Europe into East and West, were undone.

In 1918, then, under Allied directive, the Kingdom of Serbs, Croats, and Slovenes, otherwise known by the more inclusive name of the Kingdom of Yugoslavia ("of the southern Slavs"), was established under King Peter I of the Serb Karadjordjević dynasty. This included territories of Bosnia, Croatia, Macedonia, Montenegro, Serbia, and Slovenia, now joined for the first time in a common political and administrative structure but one that very soon had no political autonomy. In 1929, Alexander I, the son of King Peter, established a dictatorship. The rise of fascism in Europe was to undo him.

On October 9, 1934, in fact, Alexander I was assassinated by a member of the fascist Croatian nationalist organization Ustasha, founded among Croatian nationalist exiles in Mussolini's Italy by Ante Pavelić in 1930.[6] Since Alexander's heir, Peter, was only ten years old and thus too young to rule, Prince Paul became Regent. Paul entered into a pact with the Axis powers in 1941, leading to an uprising in Belgrade. In March of that year, Peter II, now a young adult, ascended to the throne and denounced the Axis-Yugoslav pact. The German army invaded and dismantled Yugoslavia. Croatia became an independent state including Bosnia-Herzegovina under the leadership of the *poglavnik* (duce, führer) Ante Pavelić, who was supported by both Hitler and Mussolini. Pavelić's ultrafascist, ultra-Catholic Ustasha regime viciously persecuted Serbs, Jews, Romani (Gypsies), and Croatian antifascists, building death camps and carrying out genocidal measures.[7]

In Serbia as well, Nazi collaborators engaged in atrocious violence against Croats, Jews, and Romani. Many of these collaborators were the ferocious long-bearded Chetniks, an ultranationalist Serb counterpart to the Croatian Ustasha.[8] With the pro-Yugoslav, antinationalist Partisan victory of Marshal Tito, however, the Federal Republic of Yugoslavia, including six republics (Bosnia-Herzegovina, Croatia, Macedonia, Montenegro, Serbia, and Slovenia) and two autonomous regions (Vojvodina and Kosovo), emerged from World War II as a rapidly industrializing communist state. Tito broke with Stalin in 1948 and in 1956 developed the strategy of nonalignment, along with India's Nehru and Egypt's Nasser. Throughout the first two postwar decades, the Yugoslav

National Army (JNA) grew very strong, as did decentralized regional militias, which were developed according to Partisan military models. Furthermore, the army leadership, as well as that
of the Communist Party and the police, became strongly Serb-
dominated. These decades also witnessed the decentralization of
the thriving arms industry that had lucrative contracts with both
East and West, so that a great deal of the national arms production was now occurring in Bosnia.

Until his death in 1980, Tito adamantly opposed nationalism in
the republics and strongly forbade all its manifestations. In spite
of this, sporadic outbreaks of such sentiments occurred, in 1968,
for example, when Albanians in Kosovo held demonstrations. A
rotating federal presidency came into being after Tito's death, and
Yugoslavia entered rapid economic decline as it struggled to
meet payments to the International Monetary Fund for indus-
trialization loans contracted during the first postwar decades.
People in the republics of Slovenia and Croatia, being the most
affluent, began to resent the virtual colonization and economic
control of their regions by Belgrade. Much of the wealth of these
northern republics was drained to the Serb military machine—
the one now, today, killing non-Serbs at least partly with weapons non-Serbs have paid for. Against this background, the national census of 1974 first established "Muslim" as an "ethnic"
identity.

This is the geopolitical identity context, so to speak, against
which we may study more recent events leading directly to the
war. Since I refer to these, the significant events from the mid-
1980s on, in my theme of "facts"—though both "identities" and
"facts" would more traditionally be called "history"—I'll now in-

terrupt this chronology to present some considerations of still other identities relevant to the war and the genocide in general and genocidal rape in particular.

Topospace

Bosnian-Herzegovinian and Croatian people with whom I have spoken in Zagreb and Karlovac have told me over and over again that the most important social difference that this war brings to the fore is that between city dwellers and country dwellers. Sarajevo, in particular, stands as the model of an urban society of tolerance and multiculturalism. Stories of marriages between Serbs and Croats, Croats and Muslims, Muslims and Serbs almost always turn out to be stories of city dwellers, and thus of people whose shared class and cosmopolitan identities have proven stronger, until the war at least, than their so-called ethnic or even their religious ones.

By contrast, the country dwellers, especially those who live in eastern Croatia or western Serbia, are reputed by my informants to be ultranationalistic as a matter of tradition. The country people are the staunchest upholders of the "Great Serbia" notion, the idea that Serbia has the historic right to all territories of the southern Slav states and must avenge its devastating defeat by the Turks (read "Muslims") at the Battle of Kosovo in 1389. According to my informants, many of the original Ustasha group came from what I have begun to think of as the country culture in Croatia and, in particular, Herzegovina.[9] Likewise, many say the Chetniks are based in a country culture in Serbia and in the Krajina (one of the Serb-populated regions of Croatia). Some of the university professors—all women—I met from Sarajevo remember when the leader of the Bosnian Serbs, Radovan Karadžić, "came down from the mountains," as they say, to study psychology at the university; he was dressed in the manner of the mountain culture, and his appearance was not at all adapted to the cosmopolitanism of Sarajevo. These were the years, the early sixties, they continue, when he was publishing his ultranationalist poetry. One poem in particular stands out in the minds of several people I spoke to. In it, Karadžić prophetically speaks of his mystical mission to promote the legendary Great Serbia and cries for all that stands in his way to burn, burn, burn![10] My informants say he struck other people as a doltish shepherd. In any case, he became a psychiatrist with a Ph.D. and the charismatic leader of the most reactionary nationalist Serb elements in Bosnia. Some consider him, too, to be one of the primary architects of the genocide. He already stands accused of war crimes. In any case, his class identity remains; to urban Bosnian-Herzegovinians, Sarajevans, in particular, Karadžić, even Karadžić the epically demoniac mass murderer, will always be a lout.

Although the geographic and social conditions, or topospaces, as I call them, of country dwellers allow for less contact and thus less intermarriage than in the cities between "ethnic" and religious groups, contact and intermarriage nonetheless do occur. The cultural and class differences between city dwellers and country dwellers are thus two of the main differences operant in the countries at war, but they are not for all that a strict grid that holds in all cases. By keeping topospatial differences in mind, however, I can retain some of the impact that the initial outbreaks of violence in Croatia and Bosnia-Herzegovina had for civilians. In addition to the effects of urbanity or rurality, now there were

bullets and the knife for being "Croat" or "Muslim," and, later
on, even "Serb"—those other identities that, for all but the ardent
nationalists, had become almost secondary.

Gender

A feminist theory bumper sticker, according to Cynthia Enloe,
would read "Nothing is natural; well, almost nothing" (Enloe, 3).
This slipping slogan reminds me that, as my own thinking heads
toward the variable "almost nothing" that in fact may be considered "natural," it is of the utmost importance for me to keep the
relative values of different cultures in mind. And by different cultures I mean not only Balkan cultures as compared, say, to California ones, but also scientific culture, for example, as opposed to
critical theory culture in the United States. Later on in these
themes I shall head toward a practically irreducible spot called
"biology," which my readers are of course free to think of as
"natural" or not. For now, I remain in culture. This, then, is a
brief look at gender in the war and in readings of the war.

There is a fairly strict gender division of behavior, we could
even call it work, in this war. The soldiers are generally (but not
always) men; the office workers and the caregivers are generally
(but not always) women. The male, and masculine, soldier is the
military counterpart to the generically masculinized civilian, at
times. For example, a book entitled *Mass Killing*, prepared by the
Division of Information in Croatia's Ministry of Health, gives two
general categories of noncombatant war victims from whom testimonies are reproduced: "civilians" and "women" (Granić et al.,
192-93, 198-99).[11]

Behind the front lines, the work of cultural reproduction and
interpretive readings of the war is performed by both men and

women. Since these are for the most part not soldiers, a U.S. observer like me might be inclined to assume that their activity—cultural production—is gendered as feminine, as is most cultural production in the United States. A view more common to Europe would hesitate to make that assumption, however, for many European cultures—Italian and French, for example, as well as Czech, Hungarian, and other Eastern European cultures—attribute much more political and social value to such things as literary and cinematic production and intellectual work in general than often happens in the literature-as-entertainment-oriented United States. By doing so, however, such cultures are not necessarily valorizing "feminine" activity positively; on the contrary, such activity in these cultures is taken seriously in large part because it is gendered as masculine.

Croatian, Bosnian-Herzegovinian, and Serb-Montenegrin cultures are, it seems to me, traditional Eastern European patriarchies that, like others to varying degrees, have made a few modern adaptations in marriage choices and inheritance possibilities that minimally empower women. All three nation-states are forcefully heterosexual in their official rhetoric. In fact, discourse about any sexuality other than heterosexuality is rare even in contemporary critical work on alternative cultural manifestations (Senjković, 24-51). Much of the feminist sensibility in Zagreb, both in the Croatian and in the Bosnian-Herzegovinian groups, is what U.S. feminists might call gender-aware, but many of the Croatian and Bosnian-Herzegovinian women I met do not, as far as I can tell, make the sorts of distinction between gender and sex that characterize much U.S. feminism; that is, the essentializing category "women" is the overwhelmingly central notion in their work. This is absolutely understandable, given what a major part of that work currently is: to help survivors of genocidal rape, a crime based to a large extent precisely on the existence of just that category (see theme 5, "Remedies").

For me, and for many other feminists in the United States, gender is the encoding of behavior and social possibilities that feeds me up to the world as feminine or masculine; my gender identity is entirely culturally determined. Sexuality, on the other hand, is the encoding of the workings of my erotic desire; if I desire a member of the same sex, I am homosexual; if someone of the opposite sex, heterosexual; if both, bisexual; my sexuality is psychologically determined. Sex, finally, is my identity generally as male or female, or less often as a hermaphrodite with varied proportions of male and female characteristics; my sex is biologically determined. To much feminist thinking in the United States, categorization of persons according to gender, sexuality, and sex may vary from culture to culture, but the categories themselves will always universally inhere.

Other cultures differ from the universalizing U.S. style in this, however. In Italy, for example, significant feminist thought since the 1970s has taken its impetus from the conviction that there have always been two historical subjects, as opposed to Hegel's (male) one, and that these two subjects bear an essential sexual difference: male and female (Lonzi). The object of feminist critical elaboration, then, is not gender, which for some Italian feminists remains a characteristic of grammar and nothing more, but sex, and in particular the valorization of the essential femaleness that patriarchy has traditionally banned from historiography. In France, the foremost feminist theoretician of sexual difference between maleness and femaleness and, most significantly, within femaleness itself, is Luce Irigaray, whose early works in particular,

Speculum of the Other Woman and *This Sex Which Is Not One*, have found readerships in the United States mostly within the academy but have influenced very little the rhetoric of the National Organization for Women, for example.

I mention some characteristics of Italian and French feminisms here because these are the Mediterranean-European contexts within which I have been living as I write this and as I process the information I get from across the Adriatic. Italian feminists have been aware of much of the suffering related to the war in the Balkans since it began in 1991. To my surprise, however, most with whom I have spoken had not heard about the rape/death camps. This typical lack of information notwithstanding, however, some feminists in Italy had already distinguished themselves not only by their determined recovery work with survivors but also with their strong and unhesitant expressions of moral outrage. In Pescara, for example, a provincial town on the Adriatic coast east of Rome, a high-school classics professor proposed in 1992 that Italian women form a battalion and march into the war zones as a peace force (De Filippis).[12]

I have to admit that in my own recollection of this suggestion, which I had read in an Italian feminist magazine in the spring of 1993, I added the notion of buying arms for this battalion. Somehow a pacifist reaction has not made itself available to me yet. In any case, even this proposed women's peace march, which would involve hundreds of thousands of Italian women and thus temporarily vastly depopulate many cities just like Pescara, is based on convictions that pacifism and caregiving tendencies and talents are utterly inherent to the female sex, to women. So Italian a feminist attitude would raise many polemics in circles of U.S. feminists, pacifist or otherwise.

This "Italian" feminist attitude, however, is close to the attitudes I have found among Croatian and Bosnian-Herzegovinian women. Some share the conviction that working within notions of essential difference is the appropriate task. For the time being, in any case, this difference is of the utmost importance; in combination with "ethnic" and religious identities, sexual and gender identities often determine whether one is raped or not, whether one lives or dies.

A penultimate note on gender identities in this war has to be dedicated to the Serbs' (the Bosnian Serbs, that is, supported by the Yugoslav Army) sieges of Bihać, Maglaj, Sarajevo, Srebenica, Tuzla, and Žepa, to the Croatian army's siege of Mostar, and to the Bosnia-Herzegovina Army's siege of Nova Bila. In these six United Nations "protected areas" in Bosnia-Herzegovina, as well as in other cities and towns under siege, the facts of living under constant shelling and in conditions of grave deprivation, where there is no "front" and death finds you in the breadlines, water lines, and markets, gender roles are being radically redefined. Chores that in a patriarchal gender division of labor are traditionally assigned to women—chores, that is, having to do with domestic work and reproduction—have taken on traditional masculine values associated with heroism, risk taking, boldness, and courage. The women who, over and over again, risk death by incessant sniper fire to procure water, flour, anything for their families to eat, have gradually become notable figures of strength in the family and in the community at large. At the same time, the men who remain in the cities and are thus not at the front are rendered for that reason alone less masculine by the stringent code of patriarchy's demands. Given the conditions of existence in these cities, moreover, these men no longer enjoy one of the millennial bastions of central European male privilege: the life of the café and all its attendant benefits for business and socializing. Many men, therefore, are deprived of the activities and symbols of their traditional gender dominance, and many women are benefiting symbolically from the heroic value now attached to some traditional aspects of women's labor.

This slippage in gender identity may well have had effects on the institution of marriage, for example. It would be a mistake to assume that women in Bosnia-Herzegovina do not have careers, engage in politics, or organize to support feminist concerns. They do, across religious identities. It is also important to note that several leaders of the Bosnia-Herzegovina Army units are women. The war is providing occasions for increased numbers of women to take on more traditionally masculine roles such as soldiering. I heard of one Muslim woman whose not unreasonably terrified soldier-husband refused to return to the front after a home leave. She donned his uniform, reported for service in his stead, and was killed on her first day at arms.

Finally, I mention here what I shall write about at length further on: the relation between gender and sexual identities and the atrocities. When we study the use of rape and genocidal rape in this war, it behooves us to remember that one doesn't have to be an adult female in order to be raped. In fact, rape is used against men as well as women, against children as well as adults. This being said, however, it is also of the utmost importance to articulate the role gender identity plays in the dynamics of power that attend the commission of atrocities. Attributes of masculinity always adhere to the perpetrator, whether that person is male or female, precisely because of that person's dominance over another person or group of persons and because that person is immune from prosecution. In a patriarchy, these are masculine attributes, as any battered woman in Europe, the United States, or anywhere else knows. By the same token, then, attributes of femininity always adhere to the victim, whether female or male, precisely because of that person's subjugation to another person or group of persons and because that person has no recourse to justice. In a patriarchy, these are feminine attributes, as any batterer in Europe, the United States, or anywhere else knows. The degree to which dominance and subjugation based on gender do not automatically characterize social relations, which always involve relative empowerment, is the degree to which feminist and antiracist sensibilities have promoted human rights, equal justice, and a radical democratization of the social contract.

Theme 2

REPRESENTATION

On one of my visits to the Rome offices of the *Guardian*, the English foreign correspondent Ed Vuillamy lent me two maps of Bosnia-Herzegovina. One was a road map; it reminded me of maps of California. I could estimate by comparison, for example, that the Karlovac front line was about as far from downtown Zagreb as San Mateo is from San Francisco, or that the notorious concentration and rape/death camp Omarska was about as far from Sarajevo as Los Angeles is from San Diego.

The other map was different. It was an "ethnic" map, one that showed where Serbs or Croats or Muslims make up the majority of the local population. It also gave the percentage of the population composed of groups who are not the local majority. Pie graphs were superimposed over the territorial representation so that the whole map bulged with circles of various sizes leaping out at me. Given the extent of the genocide since the map was printed in 1992, I'm sure the pie graphs would look different today. What struck me at the time, however, wasn't the fact that such a map existed. I have often studied maps of this sort; I would be surprised if there were any regions that had not been mapped this way. No, what surprised me was the function of this map. This was no sociological survey for the purpose of study; this, for someone who might be headed into Bosnia-Herzegovina, was even more important than the road map; its purpose was to save my skin.

Even a neutral observer, as a journalist might well try to be, has a difficult time negotiating the irregular and ever-changing front lines and the numerous checkpoints set up by all the armies and militias that are parties to the conflict. Added to this is the fact that you can't easily pass from a majority Serb population in Bosnia-Herzegovina to a majority Croat one, or Serb to Muslim, or Croat to Muslim, because of the suspicion your itinerary would arouse. Having a reliable representation of "ethnic" enclaves, where these exist, is literally a matter of life and death.

This is perhaps a banal example of the terrible importance of all representational practice. I am engaged in a representational practice in this writing. I am faced, therefore, with choices of the utmost importance, for the realities I shall represent are of a highly problematic nature: they are atrocities that obliterate even the most vestigial bonds of any social contract. My challenge in representing them is to do so without repeating in any way the harm those atrocities have already perpetrated; nor must I adopt misleading forms or reproduce the dynamics of permission and prohibition, of power and subjugation those atrocities are soaked with. I will not, I have decided, tell the stories.[1]

Stories are linear narratives with tremendous social power. Storytelling evokes a community of listeners and identifies them as a community. Storytelling legitimizes its listeners as a community. Stories reassure by their own formal limitations. No story goes on forever; each finds its narrative resolution. Stories, no matter how unusual, all resemble each other formally. They follow one after another in a series that promises implicitly never to end.

As linear narratives, stories contain three elements, the noting of which may at first seem quite trivial: they have a beginning, a middle, and an end. But such formal characteristics, when analyzed for their logical, or in fact ideological, implications, are far from innocent. Any beginning, for example, implies that the information it relays, the reality it represents, is significantly related to what follows and that any other information or reality is insignificant and may just as well be left out. The middle, precisely because of its centrality, announces itself as the most important part, the historically significant event. Its position relative to the beginning implies that everything narrated from the beginning to the middle is somehow causal, in fact sufficiently causal, and leads inevitably to the event narrated at the middle. In similar fashion, the story's end appears as the inevitable and unique result of all that has come before. Linear narrative form, therefore, is far from innocent in its implications of cause and effect.

Closure, the amount of things included in the story, the thickness of the representational line, so to speak, also implies cause and effect. To mention but three examples of traditional narrative technique: whatever interior details or landscapes or dialogue are included in the narrative are implicitly necessary and causal in relation to all else in the story and to the story's effect on the reader or listener. These considerations, traditionally called "style," are as far from innocent as are those we call "form."

Most important, however, linear narrative creates order. Both by its "form" and its "style," a narrative offers a package. Even the ultimate disorder of death can be ordered—that is, controlled, disciplined, and dominated—by a murder mystery, for example.

Even the vast disorder of war, shiftings of empire, and remappings of domination can be made to seem ordered by the linear narratives of traditional historiography. And even genocidal rape, which, along with other atrocious tortures, utterly negates any possible social contract, may be given the odor of order if narrated in linear fashion.

A second grave consideration regarding the representation of atrocities in general and genocidal rape in particular has to do with the effects of telling stories in a series. Since there are so many cases of genocidal rape coming out of this war, writers have often succumbed to the temptation of representing them in collected volumes (Doni and Valentini; "Pašić"). But to do so means to repeat many of the interpersonal dynamics of the crime, if not, clearly, the crime itself.

A repetitive serial form may easily hook even a reader disgusted by the events the text relates into wondering at least what comes next. This scene was so horrible, can the next one possibly be worse? And so the reader may keep turning the pages, caught in spite of her or his revulsion in the formal pleasure of repetitive linear narrative. Such narrative irrevocably places the reader in the position of voyeur.

This complicitous positioning is precisely what I want to avoid. So does the survivor, Jadranka Cigeli, who, though she has not written about her experiences in the notorious concentration camp Omarska, has spoken about them very publicly (Gutman, 144-49). Willing to testify in the international media, and therefore to risk death even as she is now at work directing the Croatian Information Office in Zagreb, this Croatian activist told me that she has not ever told the full details of what happened to her in Omarska because to do so would be to repeat that violence, at some level, on her listeners.[2]

Although the representation of genocidal rape by storytelling, or linear narrative, does not inflict permanent physical trauma or enforce pregnancy or kill its consumers, it does nonetheless reinstitute the power dynamic that obtains in the act of rape itself and in the act of observation of rape. Often, books written in sincere horror and with the laudable intention of participating in the struggle against genocidal rape and other atrocities, books that contain information valuable to anyone seeking to understand and to abolish such crimes, fall into the narrative trap. The fallacy that storytelling is innocent and therefore can be used to convey the horror of war crimes and genocide to a paying audience with no deleterious side effects is one that journalists in particular find difficult to abolish. Often, accounts of atrocities written by such professionals bear all the earmarks of the well-wrought article, with quotable phrases, easily pulled-out headlines, and so on. Readers who enter such realms of representation are warned to be on the lookout for their own complicity in another's dire suffering.

One instance of story manipulation stands out in particular. In October 1993, a book entitled *Violentate* (which would translate as "raped women") was published in Italy. The author's name, "Ehlimana Pašić," indicated that she was a Bosnian-Herzegovinian Muslim woman. The stories inside, implicitly the inside stories, in fact, were apparently those of herself and other survivors of genocidal rape, women who had confided in her as a sister victim. In fact, no such woman as Ehlimana Pašić exists. This book is a compilation of survivors' testimonies retold as stories by two male journalists from the Sarajevo newspaper *Oslobodjenje* who evidently assumed that their words would have a greater ring of truth if they appeared to come directly from a survivor than if they revealed their own presence as transcribers, or even as re-writers.

Their book leaves me very uneasy. I understand and empathize with the urgent need to tell the world about genocidal rape, about Serb rape/death camps, about ongoing atrocities. Yet I feel sad and angry that these men, whatever their intentions, took the words from the real survivors, made them over into a writing that was theirs, and then presented them as if they belonged not to a real woman but to an invented one. There are enough real women who have suffered genocidal rape not to have to invent a fictive one. Anonymity can be preserved in other ways. A more honest approach would have been for the journalists to identify them-selves and state how they had obtained their information. My un-ease turns to outrage.

Not all concerned women feel as I do, however. In fact, at the "Donne con le donne oltre l'Adriatico" (Women with women be-yond the Adriatic) conference in Rome in November 1993, *Vio-lentate* was sold to participants, and a well-known Italian actress took the stage during the opening session to do a dramatic read-ing from its pages. When she got to a part about "and she wasn't wearing any panties," I tried to stop listening. You don't have to be against erotic representation in general to be horrified by its appearance in such a context.

Numerous survivors have testified that rapes in Bosnia-Herze-govina and Croatia are routinely videotaped. This amateur por-nography production is in keeping with what may be a general-ized pornographic war use of erotic photos of women—inside

bunkers, for example (MacKinnon, 28, illustration)—as stimu-
lants for the rapists. An international pornography market awaits
whatever videotapes of genocidal rape might be coming from
the Balkans. According to one report, they have turned up in Los
Angeles.[3]

In the summer of 1993 I met a young woman on the Stanford
campus who had just returned from a year of studying in Egypt.
We got to speaking about our respective work, and I mentioned
that I had recently heard about the existence of such videotapes.
At this she became somber and pulled from her memory a recollection of something she had heard in Egypt. Friends traveling
down from Central Europe reported having seen one of these videotapes. She had been incredulous, or perhaps had experienced
the cognitive difficulties I myself encountered when I first learned
of such atrocities. She had blocked this bizarre report from her
memory, but now her affirmation reinforced my own suspicions.

It is easy to understand why persons who have been subjected
to such treatment might wish never again to be photographed.
This and other wishes of the survivors must be respected above all
else, lest their tortures be prolonged by those who aim to help
their recoveries. All people who have joined in the responsibility
of informing the world about these and other war crimes must
gauge the efficacy of their reports against the risks of representation. The sole final authorities are the survivors themselves.

Others, like myself, have relative degrees of authority to write
and say what we do. In any case, any representational authority
that accrues to someone who has not experienced these atrocities
must derive from that person's proximity to the witness of those
who have. Therefore, caregivers, observers delegated by international organizations, journalists, and other intellectuals who do

investigate and do test their sources have varying derivative degrees of authority to represent the crimes. In particular, however, such persons, and I am among them, must never intrude upon any survivor's choice to remain silent. The silence of the victim may be an integral part of her or his healing. For women, it may also be a cultural imperative, given the traditional—and transcultural—patriarchal devalorization of women who have survived rape. It may also imply her lack of trust in me, or just plain fatigue. If there is any doubt in my mind, I am obliged by all the solidarity I feel with her to assume that the reason for her silence is her own well-being. She is not obliged to tell me, or anyone else, anything, or to allow herself to be looked at, gazed upon, or studied in any way.

Self-representation by survivors need not always occur as testimony. If conditions are right, it can also take the form of analysis. At the invitation of Grytzko Mascioni, director of the Italian Institute of Culture in Zagreb, and with the generous help of Kareta and Nona (a feminist multimedia center in Zagreb), I organized an international conference in May 1994 entitled "Women, Culture, War." This proved to be a remarkable moment for the Bosnian-Herzegovinian, Croatian, Italian, and U.S. women who participated. In a rich weave of trilingual translations, we participants, whose expertise ranged through the fields of architecture, art history, feminist theory, jurisprudence, literary theory, media studies, poetry, political science, and video, spent two days in an atmosphere of intense intellectual work and attendant emotions. Our presentations elicited heated responses from an international public. After our sessions, women who had lost sons and husbands, women who were living in refugee apartments, women whose lives had been utterly undone by the aggression stood and spoke, one after the other, giving brief résumés of their experience by way of introduction but generally addressing the ethical, moral, and theoretical issues the war brings up. After the final session, one of the younger participants of whom I am particularly fond offered the criticism that the conference had been too much like an academic event, a bit too formal; we should have had a roundtable, no prepared papers, just talked to each other in order to arrive at analysis.

All too aware of the shortcomings of my efforts, and exhausted after the intellectual and organizational work, I recognized the validity of her criticism and felt crushed. Two hours later, at an end-of-conference party at Nona, this same young woman came up to me again. She told me that she had been speaking with the other Bosnian-Herzegovinian and Croatian participants. Some of them, like her, had felt coerced by the conference deadlines into writing their presentations at a moment when they might have been doing more direct relief work. Some of them had not felt confident that they would be able to produce significant analytic and theoretical papers. Once the conference was over, however, they agreed that it had been very important for them. They never would have done this work had it not been for the conference. Now they knew they could do it, and this had changed their view of themselves. It had authorized them in a world that values testimony as the voice of the body and analysis and theory as the voice of the brain—where the brain is necessarily more valuable (and by definition more male).[4]

Such representational concerns as these raise once again the issue of the original—and any other—testimonies as narratives. The testimonies the survivors provided back in 1992 avoid the pleasures of textual voyeurism and readerly delight in story format because they contain absolutely no elements of suspense, no narrative buildup, climax, and release. Even when they relate a chronology of atrocity, their tone and their point of view are those that accrue to lived experience, where everything has already happened and expectations are possible only outside the closure of the testimony.

This is one aspect of the tragedy of genocidal rape. As one of my Zagreb translators, herself a major caregiver activist, said in a moment of fatigue and secondary trauma, "These women's lives are all past and no future."[5] This is not true, of course. The present and the future are precisely the urgent concerns of survivors. As regards the recounted past time of testimony, however, there could be no greater guard against narrative suspense.

How, then, can I, an empathizing outsider, communicate what is happening without reinforcing the damage that has already been done, the damage that is being done even as I write? I have chosen to forgo storytelling except when the stories I tell are my own, what has happened to me in this subjectively limited journey toward information and a demand for justice. But I feel it is also urgently necessary to communicate the gravity of the situation. Therefore, to inform you about the atrocities, I will list them. I warn you that reading even my list will likely cause you to react emotionally—at least I hope so, for your sake. An Italian artist under the first shock of this information said to me that it was terribly disturbing and depressing, that it left him stunned, not knowing what to do, that it plunged him into deep sadness, shock, and anger. Yes, I said, I understand. And sometimes it is necessary to feel terrible in order to remain sane. Then you must act.

Please think about your reactions, therefore, and cull them for what may lead you to action, discarding any aspects of them that allow you to feel safe the way the comforting distancing of a horror story might—precisely because it's a story, and not real. Never comfort yourself with the thought that because the worst things imaginable are happening to those other people, they cannot happen to you.

I must, in fact, never forget that rape, and perhaps even genocidal rape, is not something that happens only "there," only in war, only to "them." Rape happens wherever fear and insecurity are joined with power and immunity from prosecution in a sexist social system. It happens in U.S. living rooms as well as in Serb rape/death camps. Robin Morgan has written that the fear of rape is the universal element of women's identity under patriarchy. I would modify that to read that fear of rape is the universal element of the identity of anyone gendered as feminine under patriarchy. Jadranka Cigeli told me that the rapes she suffered are different from other, "ordinary" rapes. I agree. They have become a system of femicide, to borrow Asja Armanda's apt description once again. But all rape is related in that it derives from a system of dominance and subjugation that allows, and in fact often encourages, precisely the violent crime of rape as a way of maintaining that system. I must remember the horrible difference genocidal rape makes in order to understand the particular suffering it causes and to work for an immediate end to it and then for the adequate prosecution and punishment of its perpetrators. I must also remember that it has elements of commonality with rape that happens elsewhere and in peacetime so that I will not locate all the horror of rape "over there," with "those people," as if it could never happen here, wherever here may be.

Survivors here or there may choose to tell their stories or not.

And if they do, then my obligation out of solidarity is to facilitate that choice with the greatest respect. I will not cite many of the testimonies I draw upon here, for example, and in fact I will not quote any of my survivor informants directly. This is both to safeguard them by leaving their words in a kind of documentary limbo and to safeguard the use of their accounts as official testimonies to be submitted as proof in cases that will come before the United Nations International Criminal Tribunal. Such apparent unconcern for proper scholarly standards of source documentation on my part is, in fact, the most stringent moral condition under which I may write what I have learned to be fact.

Theme 3

FACTS

The Aggression, the War

The noted scholar of nationalism Eric Hobsbawm has written that "no serious historian of nations and nationalism can be a committed political nationalist" because "nationalism requires too much belief in what is patently not so" (Hobsbawm, 12). He quotes Renan, the father of critical European discourse regarding nationalism, who said, "Getting its history wrong is part of being a nation" (12). Although I have been sympathetic to Hobsbawm's analysis for years, I must say that the versions of Serb nationalism that justify the ritual slaughter of hundreds of thousands of people in the name of a mythical "Great Serbia" have made Hobsbawm almost the only person I can bear to read on the topic of nationalism.

Nenad Popović, a thoughtful oppositional intellectual in Zagreb, considers the Serb aggression in a particular way.[1] It is, he says, a military aggression performed in the name of an extremist nationalist mythos but without the foundation even of a nation-state. In other words, the Serb military, the Bosnian Serb soldiers,

41

and the Chetniks are united in their cause, which they justify by a
bloody form of nationalism even though they enjoy little or no
functional state-based authority. In fact, the Belgrade government, continues Popović, is a fluke government voted into power
by a manipulated electoral body in an election in which only a
part of the electorate (which in any case does not include two mil-
lion Kosovo Albanians!) went to the polls. Not used to democratic
institutions, the Serbs who did bother to vote accomplished
something that, in the United States, would have been like elect-
ing candidates from the Ku Klux Klan to the presidency and to
majorities in the House and Senate.

Given this political reality, the nature of the war itself emerges
as utterly eclectic, according to Popović. With its dizzying array of
means, from the knife to rape to starvation to the smart bomb,
from orders by fax to orders by scream, from well-fed international negotiations between well-dressed British lords and well-
maned Serb war criminals in Geneva to the boiled potatoes and
chilblains of the refugee camps, this war turns out to be, in addition to everything else, also the ultimate in citational practice, in
historical collage. Not even the borders of the fighting and the
slaughter can be said to correspond to national territories of
memory. Instead, they derive from the blood-cloudy mists of extremist Serb nationalist legend. This eclectic reality, this mortal
sea of paradox, this undoing of history in the name of brute aggression, is truly a postmodern war.

It is also a genocide. Let me emphasize that, in speaking of
genocide, I am speaking precisely of a Serb policy. I have defi-
nitely taken sides. It is clear to me that the Yugoslav Army, the
Bosnian Serbs, the Chetniks, and the Belgrade government are the
aggressors in an illegal international aggression in which they aim

to take territory belonging to two internationally recognized sovereign states, Bosnia-Herzegovina and Croatia. I realize that rapes and other atrocities have been committed by Croatian, Bosnian-Herzegovinian, and United Nations forces. But, to my knowledge, none of these forces has an official policy that not only permits but recommends and commands that atrocities, including genocidal rape, be committed as the means for furthering a military and political goal: the establishment, on territory that belongs to Croatia and to Bosnia-Herzegovina, of a so-called Great Serbia justified by legend and the sort of lies and historical errors Renan and Hobsbawm lament.

The Commission of Experts appointed in October 1992 by Boutros Boutros-Ghali "to examine and analyze information gathered with a view to providing the Secretary-General with its conclusions on the evidence of grave breaches of the Geneva Conventions and other violations of international humanitarian law committed in the territory of the former Yugoslavia" draws the same conclusion. In its report to the secretary-general of the United Nations (a report I shall call the Bassiouni Report), this commission, chaired by Professor Cherif Bassiouni, describes the relative responsibility and guilt in the various war crimes and, in particular, in the widespread genocide that accompany this war. Quoting from its first interim report (S/25274), the commission describes "ethnic cleansing" as follows:

55. The expression "ethnic cleansing" is relatively new. Considered in the context of the conflicts in the former Yugoslavia, "ethnic cleansing" means rendering an area ethnically homogenous by using force or intimidation to remove persons of given groups from the area. "Ethnic cleansing" is contrary to international law.

56. Based on the many reports describing the policy and practices conducted in the former Yugoslavia, "ethnic cleansing" has been carried out by means of murder, torture, arbitrary arrest and detention, extra-judicial executions, rape and sexual assaults, confinement of civilian population in ghetto areas, forcible removal, displacement and deportation of civilian population, deliberate military attacks or threats of attacks on civilians and civilian areas, and wanton destruction of property. Furthermore, such acts could also fall within the meaning of the Genocide Convention.

The Bassiouni Report goes on to analyze the cultural forces that motivate this genocide:

130. Upon examination of reported information, specific studies and investigations, the Commission confirms its earlier view that "ethnic cleansing" is a purposeful policy designed by one ethnic or religious group to remove by violent and terror-inspiring means the civilian population of another ethnic or religious group from certain geographic areas. To a large extent, it is carried out in the name of misguided nationalism, historic grievances, and a powerful driving sense of revenge. This purpose appears to be the occupation of territory to the exclusion of the purged group or groups. This policy and the practices of warring factions are described separately in the following paragraphs.

131. With respect to the practices by Serbs in Bosnia and Herzegovina and Croatia, "ethnic cleansing" is commonly used as a term to describe a policy conducted in furtherance of political doctrines relating to "Greater Serbia." The policy is put into practice by Serbs in Bosnia and Herzegovina and Croatia and their supporters in the Federal Republic of Yugoslavia. The political doctrine consists of a complex mixture of historical claims, grievances and fears and nationalistic aspirations and expectations, as well as religious and psy-

chological elements. The doctrine is essentially based on ethnic and religious exclusivity and the dominance of Serbs over other groups in certain historically claimed areas. These views contrast with ethnic and religious pluralism. This doctrine breeds intolerance and suspicion of other ethnic and religious groups and is conducive to violence when it is politically manipulated, as has been the case.

132. It should be emphasized that this policy and the manner in which it is carried out is supported only by some Serbs. In addition, the Commission emphasizes that responsibility for criminal conduct must be determined on an individual basis.

After several paragraphs describing the means used to accomplish this "ethnic cleansing," the Bassiouni Report addresses the issue of systematic genocide as a particularly Serb practice, noting that there are many reasons to believe that the directives for it have been established at the highest levels:

142. There is sufficient evidence to conclude that the practices of "ethnic cleansing" were not coincidental, sporadic or carried out by disorganized groups or bands of civilians who could not be controlled by the Bosnian-Serb leadership. Indeed, the patterns of conduct, the manner in which these acts were carried out, the length of time over which they took place and the areas in which they occurred combine to reveal a purpose, systematicity and some planning and coordination from higher authorities. . . .

143. The above-mentioned factors and others indicate the existence of an element of superior direction. At the very least, they indicate a purposeful failure by superiors to prevent and punish the perpetrators once their crimes become known to the responsible commanders.

Regarding relative responsibility and guilt, the Bassiouni Report notes:

147. "Ethnic cleansing" practices committed by Bosnian Croats with support from the Republic of Croatia against Bosnian Muslims in Herzegovina are politically related. Furthermore, Croatian forces also engage in these practices against Serbs in the Krajina area and in eastern and western Slavonia. The violence committed against Serbs in these areas appears, however, to have the more defined political aim of removing them from the areas. Croats have used the Croatian Defence Council, police, armed civilians and local special forces to carry out these acts in the areas mentioned above. They have committed grave breaches of the Geneva Conventions, including the destruction of Serb villages and churches, killing of innocent civilians, torture and forceful removal of the civilian population. In the Krajina area and in eastern and western Slavonia, the cycle of violence between Serbs and Croats started in the early part of 1991, before the war formally began. The violence continued well beyond the end of that war. Similar practices were also, on occasion, carried out by Croats against Muslims in Bosnia and Herzegovina. But, the Croatian authorities have publicly deplored these practices and sought to stop them, thereby indicating that it is not part of the Government's policy.

148. Bosnian Government forces have also committed the same type of grave breaches of the Geneva Conventions against Serbs and Croats, but not as part of a policy of "ethnic cleansing." The number of these violations, as reported, is significantly less than the reported violations allegedly committed by the other warring factions.

Later, in a discussion of the rapes that have been used to accomplish genocide, the Bassiouni Report states unequivocally that the massive responsibility for such atrocities lies with Serb perpetrators:

251. Rape has been reported to have been committed by all sides to the conflict. However, the largest number of reported victims have been Bosnian Muslims, and the largest number of alleged perpetrators have been Bosnian Serbs.

A further paragraph reiterates the systematic, policylike nature of what I call genocidal rape:

252. In Bosnia, some of the reported rape and sexual assault cases committed by Serbs, mostly against Muslims, are clearly the result of individual or small group conduct without evidence of command direction or an overall policy. However, many more seem to be a part of an overall pattern whose characteristics include: similarities among practices in non-contiguous geographic areas; simultaneous commission of other international humanitarian law violations; simultaneous military activity; simultaneous activity to displace civilian populations; common elements in the commission of rape, maximizing shame and humiliation to not only the victim, but also the victim's community; and the timing of rapes. One factor in particular that leads to this conclusion is the large number of rapes which occurred in places of detention. These rapes in detention do not appear to be random, and they indicate at least a policy of encouraging rape supported by the deliberate failure of camp commanders and local authorities to exercise command and control over the personnel under their authority.

253. These patterns strongly suggest that a systematic rape policy existed [sic] in certain areas, but it remains to be proven whether such an overall policy existed [sic] which was to apply to all non-Serbs. It is clear that some level of organization and group activity was required to carry out many of the alleged rapes.[2]

These are some of the conclusions reached by Bassiouni and his team of experts after two years of study including numerous on-site investigations. In spite of several significant differences between the terms the report uses and those I and others who pay more specific attention to the function of gender and sex in these atrocities use, the statements in the 1994 United Nations report support the conclusions I was already reaching, with M. and many others, back in 1992.

In 1991, the first survivors of Serb rape camps began to make their way to Zagreb, leading to the collection of the testimonies M. showed me a year later. By 1992, then, many of us who knew about these things began to piece things together and to see a pattern.[3] Only slowly, however, would the factual chronology spell itself out.

The Serb Academy of Arts and Sciences "Secret" Memorandum

In 1986, six years after the death of Marshal Tito, a document often referred to as a "secret memorandum" (Weinberg and Wilsnack; *Dialogue*) was authored by Dobrica Cosić, a staunch political ally of the Serb president, Slobodan Milošević, and other members of the Serb Academy of Arts and Sciences. The "memorandum" was published by the Zagreb magazine *Naše Teme* (1989, nos. 1-2; Roux, 230), and reprinted in the collection *Izvori velikosrpske agresiji* (The origins of Serb aggression), edited by August Česareć and Školska Knjiga and published in Zagreb in May 1991 (ibid.).[4] Many of those who have written about this ideological effort on the part of Serb academicians (imagine the French Academy issuing such a memorandum!) consider it an official statement that the plan for establishing a "Great Serbia" necessitates taking the territory of the southern Slav nations, in revenge for the 1389 Battle of Kosovo. I read it somewhat differently. For me, it is a confused, racist rallying cry based on conflicting notions of nationalism: on the one hand, it says that nationalism is what has caused the current crisis, the economic and cultural oppression of Serbs throughout the Yugoslavia of the 1980s (Accademia Serba delle Scienze e delle Arti, 242); on the other, it says that the crisis perpetrates an ongoing campaign against Serb nationalism (ibid., 243).[5]

The "memorandum" calls for a revision of the Yugoslav constitution in the direction of greater regional autonomy, which, according to its reasoning, would allow for a regional levying of taxes and increased local jurisdiction, among other things. With all the clarity of hindsight, my own reading begins to see the skeleton of a plan for military aggression and even genocide in some passages that appear near the end of the "memorandum," couched in a call for regional autonomy that ostensibly would benefit all the republics:

> The revision of this constitution is an inevitable requirement in order to satisfy Serbia's legitimate interests. The autonomous provinces [Kosovo, Vojvodina] must in fact become constituent parts of the Serb Republic. They must be granted a degree of autonomy that does not place into question the integrity of the Republic and that guarantees the realization of the general interests of the enlarged community. . . .
>
> The unresolved question of the *status* of the Serb State is not the only defect that must be remedied by constitutional changes. With the 1974 Constitution, Yugoslavia became a rather flexible state community. Internally, thought has been given to various alternatives that are not solely Yugoslav, as recent declarations by Slovene leaders and Macedonian politicians' earlier positions clearly dem-

onstrate. Such reflections and a profound breakdown lead to the idea that Yugoslavia is threatened by the danger of an even greater disintegration. *The Serb people can not calmly await the future in this uncertainty. For this reason, all the nations in Yugoslavia must have the possibility of affirming their own aspirations and intentions. Thus, Serbia would itself be able to determine and define its national interest. Negotiations leading to an agreement must precede constitutional revision. Naturally, Serbia should not take a passive position, waiting simply for what others will say, as has repeatedly happened up until today.* (Accademia Serba delle Scienze e delle Arti, 244; translation and emphasis mine)

Given the Serb aggression and genocide that have followed this and other arguments for "autonomy," it is impossible for me to see here even a smidgen of democratic, fair-play, regional equivalence—or, for that matter, even of the self-serving federalism that we find in something like Italy's Northern League. The constant recourse to the notion of a Serb "people" who have a "national interest" and must not take a "passive position" clearly supports a reading of this as part of a paper trail to be used one day in attempts at justifying what in fact is a grossly illegal military aggression.

Purges: The Beginnings of Genocide

At about this same time—1986—the purge of non-Serbs had begun within the Yugoslav National Army. This purge was a racist pogrom that would pass into the world's vocabulary with the by now almost domesticated epithet "ethnic cleansing." It was conducted at first according to all the nasty, petty means of campaigns of delegitimation anywhere: nonadvancement for non-Serbs, cuts in pay, nonrecognition or misrepresentation of

achievement, increased workloads, misleading or waylaid com-
munications, and the like.

It was also being conducted by much more violent means.
Non-Serb engineers (such as my Sarajevo sociologist informant's
husband) on military assignment abroad, for example, would
meet with bizarre fatal accidents. There was almost never enough
hard evidence to prove the malicious Serb orchestration of such
apparently isolated events. But then something else began happening. Sons called to military service from middle-class urban
and also from farming families—those who were not Serbs, that
is—began having serious accidents during basic training. In fact,
they began "returning home in caskets," as one Zagreb mother
who lost her son this way told me.

The number of dead recruits was finally great enough to make
it clear that the military murder of non-Serbs within the "national" army was systematic and genocidal. Mothers in Zagreb,
including many who had lost their children to this ghastly practice, formed the group Bedem ljubavi (wall of love) and went to
Belgrade. There they demonstrated in front of the seat of government for the right to withhold their remaining sons from the
draft, both to protect their sons' lives and to prevent their sons,
should they survive the increasingly frequent boot-camp "accidents," from fighting against or otherwise harming their own
neighbors by being drafted into a Serb-serving war. I have seen
photographs of this courageous demonstration in Belgrade: the
mothers were manhandled, beaten, arrested, and sent back to
Zagreb.

In the late fall of 1987 I went to Ljubljana, the capital of Slovenia, to give a talk at an international conference on Pasolini, the
Italian filmmaker, novelist, poet, and social critic. In the company

of the Italian painter Giuseppe Zigaina, the actor Ninetto Davoli, the Italian film historian Gian Piero Brunetta, and the Dutch film critic Dorie Birkenhager, I spent a delightful few days working with Slovene intellectuals, including the poet Andrej Medved, filmmakers, novelists, journalists, and scholars. I remember vividly a long, wintry afternoon spent in what during the Austro-Hungarian Empire had been a hunting lodge in the hills overlooking the gracious city. My fantasy, inspired by the huge stuffed deer heads on the wall, imagined sleighs, endless meals, roast meats, fine wines, and the baroque finery of a middle-European ruling class in, say, the early part of the nineteenth century, led me to a world where wintry nights held poetry and candles, and where social refinements were the setting for intense passions, and of course where everyone got to live like this. Fairy-tale stuff. How far I was from the political reality, even in liberal Slovenia, then enjoying its own "Prague Spring."

A couple of months after my return to Stanford, I received a letter from Dorie Birkenhager saying that she had been having no luck whatsoever reaching the people who had organized our Pasolini conference. Worse, some newspaper articles that had recently appeared in Dutch papers suggested that some sort of Belgrade-run pogrom against wayward Slovenian intellectuals might be under way, and she sent the articles along for me to peruse. Since I couldn't read Dutch and didn't know anyone who could, I felt mightily frustrated and deeply worried. Then one day, as I was locked into a particularly long stretch of freeway on the Bay Area peninsula, I heard an interview on the Berkeley Pacifica radio station, KPFA. A woman from Ljubljana was telling us that, yes, a plot had been unearthed in Yugoslavia whereby a secret directive had gone out from Belgrade ordering the arrest, detention, *and execution* of a group of Slovene intellectuals in Ljubljana! The directive had been discovered in time for these intellectuals to go into hiding or leave the country, and, as a consequence, none of them had been arrested. Subsequently, orders from the very top level of the government in Belgrade had canceled the directive, condemning it as being, in fact, a mistakenly independent initiative on the part of officials who had not bothered to obtain official approval from the highest ranks in the state. Stuck there on the freeway, I had not heard the name of the person being interviewed and, although I spoke about this incident with many people in the United States and Italy for months thereafter, none of its logic was to become clear to me until much later. Now it is clear that such behavior coming out of Belgrade coincides with the genocidal murders in the armed forces and the elimination of non-Serbs from positions of authority in that and other institutions. Now—now that it is too late, that is—it is easy to see how the spittle-coated moniker "ethnic cleansing" was taking on meaning long before it was to hit the international media and give the "international community" something to shake its collective head over at news time.

Independence and Aggression: A War Chronology

In 1990, each of the republics in Yugoslavia holds its first free parliamentary elections. The atmosphere of liberalization from the centralized totalitarian regime heightens populist nationalist feelings everywhere. In Slovenia, the reformist Milan Kučan is elected to the presidency; in Croatia, the nationalist Franjo Tudjman; and in Belgrade, the ultranationalist Slobodan Milošević. At the end of the year, Slovenia holds a plebiscite, which results in its call for secession from the state of Yugoslavia.

At about this time, the Republic of Croatia adopts as its own a medieval crest, a slightly varied version of what had once been the Ustasha flag. This symbol of earlier vicious anti-Serb (and anti-Jew, anti-Romani, and anti-antifascist) repression now becomes the official symbol of the Croatian republic, causing many Serbs living in Croatia to feel fearful, whether such fear is justified or not. In fact, on March 3, 1991, a band of Serbs living in Pakrac (in Croatia) occupies several public buildings, takes possession of police armaments, and engages in armed fighting with the Croatian militia. On March 30, another armed conflict between Croatian Croats and Croatian Serbs takes place, this time before the terrified eyes of hundreds of tourists in the Plitvice national park. The army intervenes, bringing the fighting to a halt. In this part of Croatia's Krajina, which is inhabited by a large Serb population, the regional authorities declare secession from Croatia and union with Belgrade, a declaration that will be sanctioned by a regional referendum on May 12.

Spring 1991 in Croatia grows bloodier with the massacre of twelve Croatian policemen by Serb guerrillas in Borovo Selo. Then, the next day, Croats take vengeance by attacking Serb-owned stores in Zara. "Ethnic" identities are beginning to assert themselves in territorial pockets beyond the regions nominally associated with those identities. The cultural tolerance that for centuries characterized life in the southern Slav states is beginning to give way to legendary nationalist claims of Serb right to Croatian territory.

On May 19, a Croatian referendum calls overwhelmingly for independence and, on June 25, both Slovenia and Croatia declare themselves to be sovereign states. Now begins the war in Slovenia, the "short" war, officially declared by General Blagoje Adžić on

July 2. On July 27, the Yugoslav National Army (already "ethni-cally cleansed" and thus Serb-run) intervenes, and a bloodbath begins in the countryside. After thirteen days of fighting, and with the intervention of the European Community, the parties declare a three-month moratorium on Slovenian as well as Croat-ian independence. An international committee helps to negotiate a cease-fire in Slovenia and, by the end of the three-month mora-torium, the "national" (Serb) army has left Slovenia.

Things get much worse slightly to the south. In Zagreb, Tudj-man calls on residents of Croatia to be prepared for war and, on July 24, he requests the intervention of UN peacekeeping troops. By mid-August, resistance to Serb uprisings has begun through-out Croatia. Bombs launched by Serbs (the Croatians had no bombs at the time) destroy the freeway between Zagreb and Bel-grade. Tudjman gives the Yugoslav National Army an ultimatum: either stop supporting Serb irregulars in Croatia or the Zagreb government will consider your presence in Croatia an invasive occupation. By mid-September the fighting has reached the Dal-matian coast and even up to Fiume. On October 1, the Serb ir-regulars and the Yugoslav National Army begin the siege of the beautiful Croatian seacoast town of Dubrovnik. One week later, they bomb the heart of the old city in Zagreb.

Then, on October 8, the three-month moratorium ends, and both Slovenia and Croatia declare their independence. A little more than a month later, on November 17, an astonishingly de-structive Serb (read Chetnik, and irregular Serb militia, and Yugo-slav National Army) ninety-one-day siege costing thousands of lives finally causes the fall of Vukovar, "symbol," as Gigi Riva and Marco Ventura put it, "of the Croatian resistance in Slavonia" (the eastern part of Croatia) (Riva and Ventura, 11).

Serb Documents Ordering and Confirming Genocide and Genocidal Rape

During this late-summer and early fall bloodletting in 1991, some ominous documents were being prepared in Belgrade. Italian journalists with whom I have spoken have seen photographs of the minutes of the meetings at which these documents were ratified; the information I give here is based on my acceptance of the validity of their eyewitness claims. The first is called the Ram Plan, and it is written, while war rages in Croatia, by the following Serb army officers: General Blagoje Adžić (formerly commander in chief of the Yugoslav Army and chief of military security), General Major Milan Guero, Major Čedo Knežević, Lieutenant Colonel Radenko Radinović, and General Alexandar Vasiljević (successor to Adžić as commander in chief). This is the first official document establishing "ethnic cleansing" as military policy.

The Italian journalist Giuseppe Zaccaria dates the Ram Plan from the later part of 1991, probably the end of August (Zaccaria, 125). Interpreting the minutes from the meeting the Yugoslav Army officers held in the suburbs of Belgrade in late 1991 in order to decide whether the Ram Plan was still workable, Zaccaria writes:

> Essentially they are about a military plan that, in the case of secessionist movements, foresees the [Serb] occupation of Croatian territory and Bosnia-Herzegovina, the movement of [Serb] troops into the Sandjak, and the control of an area where Muslim fundamentalism might prove to be particularly strong. (A Ljubljana company formerly run by the state had already sent containers that were filled with Kalashnikovs instead of industrial equipment; the generals say that Libya has sent the money.) As far as the Krajina is

concerned, military experts will take charge of organizing the local [militia] groups in order to provoke civil unrest and "calls" for [Serb] intervention and advances. (Ibid., 127)

According to the minutes, the military strategy meeting now moves on to consider a variation of the Ram Plan written by the army's special services, including psychologists and experts in psychological warfare (ibid.) These services have determined that particular means will have to be adopted should a widespread conflict develop—should war begin, that is, with Croatia, the Krajina, and Bosnia-Herzegovina. Zaccaria now quotes from the minutes:

Our analysis of the behavior of the Muslim communities demonstrates that the morale, will, and bellicose nature of their groups can be undermined *only if we aim our action at the point where the religious and social structure is most fragile. We refer to the women, especially adolescents, and to the children.* Decisive intervention on these social figures would spread confusion among the communities, thus causing first of all fear and then panic, leading to a probable [Muslim] retreat from the territories involved in war activity.

In this case, we must add a wide propaganda campaign to our well-organized, incisive actions so that panic will increase. We have determined that the coordination between decisive interventions and a well-planned information campaign can provoke the spontaneous flight of many communities. (127-29; emphasis mine)

Zaccaria paraphrases the remaining sections of the officers' minutes. Clearly this second joint "decisive intervention" "propaganda" plan is separate from and additional to the Ram Plan; and in fact the officers now refer to it as the Brana Plan. ("Ram" means "loom"; thus the Serb military policy will weave its way

from many angles across Bosnia-Herzegovina and Croatia.
"Brana" means "dam"; thus the Serb military policy will "dam
up" the Muslim population, keep it elsewhere, keep it from the
territories Serbia wants to take.) The remaining grave problem for
the officers gathered in the Belgrade suburb in August 1991 is
whom to appoint as commander of this new *military operation
aimed at noncombatant women and children.* They agree that the
chain of command should be as small as possible; it should, they
say, resemble the "slim company" management style: light on top
(Zaccaria, 128). Within the army, Colonel Zeljko Raznjatović
should direct it. Wherever necessary (i.e., in the territories the
Serbs will soon invade), General Ratko Mladić, chief of the Bosnian Serb forces, will coordinate the efforts of such "autonomous" groups as Vojislav Šešelj's "White Eagles" and Arkan's
(Raznjatović's) "Tigers" (ibid.). These latter are two of the most
ferocious Chetnik and Serb irregular groups in Bosnia-Herzegovina; their bloodthirsty ravages have earned them reputations
that make visions of hell pale by comparison.[6]

The first indications of the existence of Serb rape/death camps
in Bosnia-Herzegovina, remember, are reaching Zagreb at just
this time, in late 1991, as survivors begin to bring their tortured
bodies and spirits for healing and their stories as testimony. M.
will begin translating some of these stories in California about
eight months later. Given the survivors' evidence, particularly
now that the Bassiouni Report has confirmed so much of it, there
is no doubt in my mind that the Ram Plan and the Brana Plan
went into effect immediately. The rhetoric of "maybe" that
Zaccaria quotes and paraphrases from the generals' meeting in
suburban Belgrade reveals itself as a hedge against eventual accu-
sations of clear aggressive intent. This rhetoric, like the 1986

"memorandum" from the Serb Academy of Arts and Sciences, bears the unmistakable odor of a putrid paper trail calculated to mislead its readers as to the actual intentions of the Serb military command. Simultaneously, it officially establishes that the illegal means of psychological terror and the genocidal targeting of civilians are now the policy of the coordinated Serb military, paramilitary, and Chetnik forces.

My literary tendencies—or my hindsight—may have gone too far in interpreting the Academy's memorandum as a clear indication of official genocidal Serb policy with distinct gender and age specifications. If this be the case, news of the Ram and Brana plans should suffice to dispel any doubts as to the Serb military policy. But Zaccaria reports that still other damning documents exist. These include a photocopy of a telegram from Arkan to the Bosnian Serb commander (Mladić), the president of Serbia (Milošević), and the commander of the Serb army (Adžić), and another photocopy of a report signed by Colonel Obradović of the Serb army. These documents report that the "cleansing" of the Bosnian territories is proceeding apace and that the psychological attack on the Muslim population in Bosnia is working well and should be continued (Zaccaria, 130).

A third photocopy is that of a letter from the commander of the third battalion of the Serb army, Milan Dedić, to the chief of the secret police in Belgrade, Mihajlo Kertes. This reads:

Sixteen hundred and eighty Muslim women of ages ranging from twelve to sixty years are now gathered in the centers for displaced persons within our territory. A large number of these are pregnant, especially those ranging in age from fifteen to thirty years. In the estimation of Boško Kelević and Smiljan Gerić, the psychological effect is strong, and therefore we must continue [the practice of genocidal rape]. (Ibid.)

Zaccaria hedges his bets on the authenticity of these documents, which he says are contained in a dossier that has been sent to the UN tribunal by the Bosnians who discovered them. But even this foreign correspondent, who has his credibility to lose if they are false, and who himself is not particularly sensitive to all the gender issues involved in these atrocious policies (his sense of propriety is sincerely offended by the manner in which the Serbs degrade Bosnian women, to whom he refers, in relation to Bosnian men, as "le loro donne" [their women] [131]), has come to this conclusion: should these documents be proved false, their very falsification is "diabolical" (ibid.) because they associate the atrocities committed by the Serbs with crimes committed by the UN forces as well. A document signed by Mihajlo Kertes (a former communist, now a nationalist, of Hungarian origin from Voyvodina) and addressed to the Serb army reads, for example:

The Yugoslav Ministry of Internal Affairs [remember that this is the Belgrade government] will open no inquests on the rapes since these constitute a part of the [army's] psychological and strategic pressure activities. In accordance with the Ministries of Health and Security, and upon the request of Dr. Vida Mandić and Colonel Loginov, it is established that a certain number of young women, the numbers to be agreed upon, will be transferred to Slavonia and Baranja for the needs of the Serb forces and also for the Unprofor [United Nations Protection Force] officers. (Ibid.)

I end my discussion of the "documents" section of Zaccaria's book by signaling the final text he cites. It's a little note signed by

Loginov (he's the Serb colonel who, along with the Dr. Mandić in the document just cited, has decided to send young Bosnian women off to be raped by Serb and UN soldiers), a little note that with one sentence illustrates the gross and blatant sexism that could have invented genocidal rape in the first place. Loginov jots this down: "I suggest we send eighty or a hundred or so girls to satisfy the officers' needs" (ibid.).

Testimony

Any difficulties I may have had in giving credence to Zaccaria's sketchily documented reports of the textual proof of genocide as official Serb military policy have been utterly erased by my conversations with survivors and by the Bassiouni Report. One of the survivors—the one who told me the history of the Bogomils—said that Sarajevans knew of the intentions of the ultranationalist Serbs long before the war began. She mentioned that she had heard a tape of a conversation that took place in the late 1980s between a former British ambassador and a colleague of hers at the University of Sarajevo, Ketzmanović, a major ideologue of the genocide. Seeing as how the West knew a war was coming, says the British ambassador, how could the crisis in Yugoslavia be overcome? The Serb extremist responds, Easy, we need to send a third of the Muslims away, convert a third of them to the Orthodox church, and kill all the rest. The person who said this was a professor of political science at the University of Sarajevo who, even though he was clearly advocating what under any circumstances would be crimes against humanity, just as clearly had nothing to fear for being so outspoken. The boldness of his declaration in an international context is yet another indication of the degree to which the plan for genocide was becoming official Belgrade policy *and the degree to which this was known internationally.*

Given these facts of past history, the chronology of the aggression, and documentary and testimonial indications of Serb genocidal military policy, including the concerted effort to destroy Bosnian-Herzegovinian and Croatian culture by attacking, in a particularly ferocious and sexist manner, women and children—those civilians least able to defend themselves (because they are sure not to be armed)—just what are the facts about genocidal rape?

Genocidal Rape

Genocidal rape is a military policy of rape for the purpose of genocide currently practiced in Bosnia-Herzegovina and Croatia by the Yugoslav Army, the Bosnian Serb forces, and the irregular Serb militia known as Chetniks. Three main forms exist: (1) Chetniks or other irregular forces enter a Bosnian-Herzegovinian or Croatian village, take several women of varying ages from their homes, rape them in public view, and depart. The news of this atrocious event spreads rapidly throughout the village. Several days later, regular Bosnian Serb soldiers or Serbs from the Yugoslav Army arrive and offer the now-terrified residents safe passage out of the village on the condition that they never return. Most accept, leaving the village abandoned to the Serbs and thus furthering the genocidal plan of "ethnic cleansing." It is hard to imagine they could do otherwise, being unarmed except for their farm implements and a rusty rifle or two. Thus the Serbs—in a collaboration between their Chetnik and their regular military forces—accomplish the rout of the Bosnian-Herzegovinian population of still another village with very little cost to themselves. The "ethnic cleansing" accomplished by this procedure is the clockwork-precise, logical putting-into-practice of the Ram and Brana plans the Serb commanders wrote in 1991; (2) Bosnian-Herzegovinian and Croatian persons being held in Serb concentration camps are chosen at random to be raped, often as part of torture preceding death; (3) Serb, Bosnian Serb, and Croatian Serb soldiers and the militias and irregular forces known as Chetniks arrest Bosnian-Herzegovinian and Croatian women, imprison them in a rape/death camp, and rape them systematically for extended periods of time. Such rapes are either part of torture preceding death or part of torture leading to forced pregnancy. Victims who do not become pregnant are often murdered. Victims who do become pregnant are raped consistently and subjected to severe psychological abuse and other forms of torture until such time as their pregnancies have progressed beyond the stage when a safe abortion would be possible, at which point they are released. All forms of genocidal rape constitute the crime of genocide as described in Article II of the 1948 United Nations Convention on the Prevention and Punishment of the Crime of Genocide.[7]

I will tell you here of Jadranka Cigeli, a Croatian woman who is divorced, as I am, from the father of her son (her former husband is Montenegrin). Jadranka, who now directs the Croatian Information Office in Zagreb, is an attorney who had gone to live in Prijedor, in northern Bosnia, where she had been active in Croatian cultural activities. Jadranka is one of the most public and consequently one of the bravest survivors of genocidal rape.[8] I met Jadranka in the fall of 1993 and spent time with her again when she participated in the international conference I organized in

Zagreb, "Women, Culture, War," in May 1994. Jadranka had been arrested in her home by Serb irregulars armed with automatic weapons and taken to the notorious Omarska concentration camp—the iron mine converted to a city of torture and starvation.[9] For six long weeks, from June 14 to August 3, 1992, Jadranka and thirty-two other women were kept locked in a rape/death camp inside Omarska. This was two rooms from which the women were taken to be raped on a regular basis. Jadranka has identified one of her rapists as Željko Mejahić, commander of the camp guards.

I asked Jadranka if she had been subjected to the particular psychological torture, amidst all the others, of hearing from her torturer/rapist that now she would give birth to a little Serb soldier, now she would bring a little Chetnik into the world. To this she replied no. The women at Omarska were never told such things, she said, because everyone, the guard rapists as well as the prisoners, knew the women would be killed. This is an example of systematic genocidal rape conducted in a rape/death camp within a concentration camp where the rapes constitute a part of the torture that precedes death.

Jadranka escaped because of what she calls the courageous risk taking and immense luck of a team of Red Cross personnel and the Norwegian ambassador, who personally accompanied the Red Cross workers into Omarska. In a ruse that brings to mind some of the boldest anti-Nazi actions of World War II, this ambassador managed to add the names of the women being held at Omarska to a list of prisoners he was authorized to bring out. Three women, however, did not get on the list, and to this day we do not know their fate. I promised Jadranka that I would speak and write of these women whenever I could. Now, therefore, I call on the

Belgrade government to announce the whereabouts and state of health of these women and any others not released from Omarska, or, if any are dead, to announce when, where, and in what manner they perished.

Rape/Death Camps

Rape/death camps are buildings where Bosnian-Herzegovinian and Croatian women and girls are kept and systematically raped for weeks or months at a time by Serb personnel from the Yugoslav Army, irregular Serb soldiers, Chetniks, and even civilians. The rape/death camps are restaurants, hotels, hospitals, schools, factories, peacetime brothels, or other buildings; they are also animal stalls in barns, fenced-in pens, and arenas. Testimony indicates that upwards of thirty such rape camps have been or are currently in use.[10]

Documentation of Genocidal Rape and Rape/Death Camps

Caregivers in Zagreb with whom I have spoken began learning about genocidal rape and Serb rape/death camps in late 1991 and early 1992. Roy Gutman began publishing reports about them in August 1992, in *New York Newsday* and the *Washington Post*. In its July-August 1993 issue, *Ms.* magazine did a cover story, "Turning Rape into Pornography: Postmodern Genocide," by Catharine MacKinnon.

By the fall of 1993, many reports of Serb genocidal rape and rape/death camps were available in the United States. On October 20 of that year, for example, the Croatian Mothers Organization came to New York to tell the world about their sons killed in Croatia. Some of these young men had been killed defending their towns. Others, having been wounded, had been taken from hospitals by Serbs or had been interrogated by Serbs and were now missing. Even these women, whose own particular interest was the fate of their sons, knew in great detail about local instances of genocidal rape and rape/death camps, particularly in Vukovar. A report on their United Nations press conference prepared by the Agora Information Service includes the following:

> Ms. Butula [Ljubica Butula, leader of the group and a professor at the University of Zagreb whose son died defending Zadar] said that some 400 women and 87 children had been taken away from Vukovar and were unaccounted for. The rape of thousands of women had been documented. The Serbs even had camps for the sole purpose of detaining women. Serbs had taken 150 Muslim women away from the town of Brčko in Bosnia and Herzegovina.[11]

Adding Scandal to Atrocity

In a just, moral world, knowing that even one person has been subjected to such treatment should be enough to guarantee immediate and effective intervention to stop it. Neither the numbers of victims nor the identities of perpetrators should check the immediacy of such a reaction. But there are aspects of this genocide that seem to add a degree of shame and disgust to what can only be described as already a maximally shameful and disgusting situation. One such degree was added to the growing U.S. press verification of these practices when, on November 1, 1993, Roy Gutman relayed that Unprofor soldiers had also been perpetrators of rape. He obtained this information from the testimony of Borislav Herak, a twenty-two-year-old Serb soldier who nine months earlier had been sentenced to death by the Bosnian-Herzegovinian government "for raping and murdering Muslim and Croat women at Sonja's [Sonja's Kon Tiki, a restaurant-rape/death camp in Vogošča, six miles north of Sarajevo]" (Gutman, 7). Herak's testimony that he had seen UN personnel at Sonja's had been reinforced by the Bosnian Serb commander of the camp during 1992, Branislav Vlaco, who told Gutman that during that time UN personnel came several times a week "for food and drinks, to watch television on his satellite receiver, 'and they came for the girls, too' " (ibid.). Vlaco also ran a bunker behind Sonja's restaurant, Gutman reports, where other prisoners, mostly male, were kept in subhuman conditions and forced to perform sexual acts on each other (7, 27).

In this same article, Gutman reports that witnesses had seen UN soldiers frequenting the Park Hotel in Vogošča, where local women who had been seized by Serb soldiers were taken to be raped. Witnesses identified the UN soldiers as Canadian, New Zealander, French, Ukrainian, and African. One of the soldiers seen frequenting Sonja's Kon Tiki is Canadian Maj. Gen. Lewis MacKenzie, who commanded the UN Protection Force in Sarajevo during 1992. MacKenzie denies this. His deputy, Col. Michel Jones, says that UN commanders "had heard of the camp at Sonja's but adds: 'It was not part of our job to visit those camps. If someone visited those camps, it was Richard Gray,' the senior military observer" (29). Gray denies visiting the Park Hotel, "but when he was reminded that Vlaco and other Serb officials said they had hosted Gray at a lunch there, Gray recalled, 'Oh, wait a minute. Now that you're bringing it back, we went to a meeting, we then went to the hotel and had a meeting there,' he said" (ibid.). At the time Gutman's article appeared, Gray was serving as the military attaché at the New Zealand UN mission in New York.

Let me emphasize that this *New York Newsday* article—written more than a year after Gutman's first mention of such things in the U.S. press—makes it very clear that Serb rape/death camps and the practice of genocidal rape were already in force in Bosnia. On page 26, after giving an initial report of the atrocities at Sonja's, Gutman writes: "These reported abuses were taking place at about the same time Serb forces were operating rape camps and systematically raping Muslim and Croat women as part of their 'ethnic cleansing' campaign to drive non-Serbs out of Bosnia."

Another U.S. press report of genocidal rape is Paul Lewis's *New York Times* article of October 20, 1993 (A1) (the same day the Croatian Mothers group was giving a press conference at the United Nations). Lewis reports that a UN war crimes commission "has found evidence that rape was used by the Serbs as a weapon of terror in the war against Bosnia and Herzegovina" and that "Muslim women were raped by Serbian soldiers as part of their campaign of 'ethnic cleansing.' " Further, Lewis reports that, "on the basis of an examination of 330 victims, the commission says it is inclined to believe that rape was used by the Serbs as a weapon of war in their campaign to drive Muslims from their homes and seize their land."

One of the most authoritative documentations of the genocidal rapes available prior to the Bassiouni Report is the United Nations General Assembly Security Council document A/48/92, S/25341, dated February 26, 1993, and entitled "The Situation of Human Rights in the Territory of the Former Yugoslavia." This document contains the fourth report prepared by the Special

Rapporteur of the United Nations' Commission on Human Rights, Tadeusz Mazowiecki, who had made several official visits to Bosnia-Herzegovina, Croatia, Macedonia, Montenegro-Serbia, and Slovenia. In almost eighty pages of single-spaced documentation, Mazowiecki and his team state with clarity and in surgical detail the profound gravity of the situation. Let me relay but a few of the moments in this ringing indictment.

In a section containing the team's report on "allegations of rape in the territory of the former Yugoslavia," Mazowiecki writes:

> 6. According to some of these sources [representatives of the governments concerned, international organizations with representation in the locations that were visited, nongovernmental organizations concerned with women's issues, local women's groups, religious leaders of Muslim communities, and other sources including Unprofor officials, relatives of detained or disappeared persons, as well as relatives of victims of rape (64)], rape has been used since the beginning of the conflict on a large scale, as a means of implementing the strategy of ethnic cleansing and to increase inter-ethnic hatred. Paramilitary groups are said to be responsible in most cases. The victims are said to be mainly Muslim but also Serb and Croat women. Most reports relate to the months of May and June 1992. Attempts made to locate specific places where women were allegedly detained and raped have proved unsuccessful to date. Information was often too imprecise. In several cases, alleged rape camps were found to be empty when visited by ICRC [International Committee of the Red Cross] delegates. (65)[12]

In the section entitled "Analysis of statistical data and medical records," the report notes that rape, which "is among the most under-reported crimes in peacetime throughout the world, . . .

continues to be under-reported during wartime" (67), mostly because victimized women feel they have no recourse. "Rape by soldiers is increasingly used as a weapon of war against women and
girls" (67).

The report continues: "24. Many women will not talk about
their experience of rape for fear of reprisals. Many women interviewed by the team of experts personally knew, or knew the
names of, the men who had raped them. Some were reluctant to
tell the experts the names of the perpetrators because of fear for
their own and their family's safety" (67).

This conclusion, reached by the team of UN experts in February 1993, reiterates what survivors who have made it to Zagreb
often say. The world press continues to paint a picture of severe
family censure, particularly of Muslim rape survivors. This is only
a partial representation. First of all, censure of raped women in a
patriarchal family derives from that family's patriarchal nature,
which is not limited to one religion. It would be a disservice to
both Muslim women and Catholic or Orthodox Christian women
to pretend either that such censure always happens in Muslim
families or that it never happens in Christian ones. In the Bosnian-Herzegovinian refugee community of Turin, for example,
there is a young Muslim family—woman, man, and two small
children—who were imprisoned in a Serb concentration camp
where the wife was subjected to genocidal rape and became pregnant. The family somehow got out and reached a refugee camp,
still in Bosnia-Herzegovina. While there, the parents sought unsuccessfully to obtain an abortion. Later, safe in Italy, and with the
prospect, though dim, of finding jobs, they decided to continue
the pregnancy and raise the child. They told an Italian friend that
their earlier decision to abort the pregnancy arose from their con-

viction that they would not have been able to care for the child financially. Once they had begun to hope for economic stability, however, they could continue the pregnancy and accept the child as their own.

As Mazowiecki notes, another reason survivors of genocidal rape often wish not to name their rapists even when they are able to do so is that they fear reprisals. These may well occur not only against family members, as the UN report suggests, but also against the women still being held in rape/death camps and concentration camps. Such reprisals are to be expected whenever outside powers or forces are awakened against the genocide. They happened on a large scale in other cities when NATO intervened to lessen temporarily the Serb siege of Sarajevo. No one knows the mortal reality of the threat better than the women themselves.[13]

Many survivors do bear witness, however. Archives of their testimonies now exist under the conservatorship of the UN Tribunal's prosecuting attorney's office. As part of his work as director of the United Nations Commission of Experts, Dr. Cherif Bassiouni has compiled a database of testimonies of over three hundred thousand war crimes, including tens of thousands of instances of genocidal rape, which he has submitted to the UN International Criminal Tribunal for the former Yugoslavia. M. is also gathering testimonies. Many groups in Zagreb are collecting still more. There can be no doubt as to the genocidal crimes. There can also be no doubt as to the fact that, on the Serb side, those crimes are *policy*.

In its "evaluation of findings," Mazowiecki's group writes:

30. It is not possible to know precisely the actual number of rapes or the number of pregnancies due to rape that have occurred. How-

ever, estimates can be made based on the 119 documented cases [available to them in 1992] of pregnancy resulting from rape. Medical studies suggest that of every 100 incidents of rape, one will result in pregnancy. This suggests that the 119 documented cases were likely to have been the result of approximately 12,000 incidents of rape. Since it is clear that women experienced multiple and/or repeated rape, this figure should not be construed as a direct indication of the number of women who were raped in the populations using the medical facilities visited by the team of experts but may only serve as a guide to the general scale of the problem. (69)

Of course not even the dedicated nonpartisan team of Mazowiecki's experts could interview the women for whom rape had been a prelude not to release, perhaps hospitalization or a refugee camp, and often pregnancy, but to death.

As far as criminal responsibility is concerned, the UN report notes occurrences of rape and even of imprisonment and rape perpetrated by Croatian and Bosnian-Herzegovinian as well as Serb forces (69-70). Details that come to the fore in the testimony of Catholic and Muslim, Croatian and Bosnian-Herzegovinian women, however, indicate once again the specific strategy of genocide that lies behind the Serb practice of rape:

40. Six Muslim and two ethnic Croat women reported having been raped [in one group of sixteen women interviewed, three of whom were what the report calls "ethnic" Croats and thirteen of whom were Muslim]. One 43-year-old Muslim woman reported being repeatedly raped in her apartment in a Serb-occupied area for seven months until she managed to escape. The perpetrators, who came to the apartment regularly two or three times a week, were two ethnic Serb neighbors in paramilitary uniforms. Another Muslim woman reported how some of the ethnic Serbs in her village

rounded up the Muslims and took them to a primary school where she was detained with 12 other women and about 400 men. "The soldiers would come every evening around midnight, drunk and dirty. This went on for about two months. Some of them were my neighbors, and some of them I did not know, from Serbia. There was a room with five or six men in it. They would all rape one woman and then take her away and bring in another woman. All 13 of us were taken there; the youngest girl was ten years old." (70)

41. One ethnic Croat woman was detained in a Serb-controlled camp with 34 other women and a large number of men. She reported that all 34 women in the camp were raped: "There were so many killings, torture. Death became very familiar. All of the women were begging to be killed, to be shot, not to be tortured. . . ." Another ethnic Croat woman was detained in a "special house" where she was raped by several men every night for approximately two months. Every night she could hear screams and cries of other women. She reported that, while raping her, the men were shouting: "you will have a Serb child." She also reported being told that, if she were pregnant, she would be "forced to stay there until six months of pregnancy." (70-71)

In reviewing documents and testimonies received, and in going over meetings with physicians who were caring for survivors, Mazowiecki and his team of experts begin to see several patterns. They note, for example:

(a) Rape has been used as one method to terrorize civilian populations in villages and forcing ethnic groups to leave. One example of this was described by a physician who interviewed several women from the region of Vukovar (Croatia). There Serb paramilitary units would enter a village. Several women would be raped in the presence of others so that word spread throughout the village and a climate of fear was created. Several days later, Yugoslav Popular Army (JNA) officers would arrive at the village offering permission to the non-Serb population to leave the village. Those male villagers who had wanted to stay then decided to leave with their women and children in order to protect them from being raped;

(b) In one pattern that was reported in several Serb-controlled areas, particularly in Bosnia and Herzegovina, local Serb forces in conjunction with Serb forces from outside the area would occupy a village and restrict the movement of the local population. Often, men were deported or fled. Women were then often raped in their own homes or taken from their homes to another location and raped, often by neighbors or people known to them. Reports of similar abuses were obtained from a Serb refugee who came from north-eastern Bosnia and Herzegovina, regarding a number of villages occupied by Croat forces, particularly in the region of Novi Grad;

(c) Although the team of experts heard stories about individuals, Croats, Muslims and Serbs, who risked their own safety to try and help their threatened neighbors, they heard of no attempts made by anyone in a position of authority to try and stop the raping of women and girls. In fact, some of those in power actively participated in it. One example for this was given by a Muslim woman living in a Serb occupied town. She reported being taken by an ethnic Serb policeman to a private home where she was presented with the words: "Here she is, Commander. I brought her!" She recognized the "Commander" as one of the strongest political figures in the region before the war. He told her to go into his office, which was his bedroom, where he raped her. Serb women also reported that women were raped by Croat and Muslim policemen and men in positions of authority;

(d) Rape was also commonplace in detention camps on all sides. There, women were kept together in rooms in a separate part of the camp. Women were taken individually to other rooms, where they would be repeatedly raped. (72-73)

In its "Conclusions" section, Mazowiecki's February 1993 UN report states:

> 59. Rape of women including minors has occurred on a large scale. While the team of experts has found victims among all ethnic groups involved in the conflict, *the majority of the rapes that they have documented had been committed by Serb forces against Muslim women from Bosnia and Herzegovina.*
>
> 60. The team of experts is not aware of any attempts by those in positions of power, either military or political, to stop the rapes.
>
> 61. There is clear evidence that Croat, Muslim and Serb women have been detained for extended periods of time and repeatedly raped.
>
> 62. *In Bosnia and Herzegovina and in Croatia, rape has been used as an instrument of ethnic cleansing.* (74; emphasis mine)

I have cited Mazowiecki's February 1993 UN report in detail because it is the most thorough document on genocidal rape that the United Nations produced prior to the Bassiouni Report. Its findings undeniably confirm that the Serb military, as well as irregular Serb forces in Bosnia-Herzegovina and Croatia, have been implementing the policy set forth in the Ram and Brana plans of August 1991. It is precisely these policies that differentiate the Serb practice of rape *as genocidal rape* from Croatian, Bosnian-Herzegovinian, and Unprofor wartime rape, as well as from peacetime rape in general; the report's conclusions recognize this difference.

The Bassiouni Report contains an extensive section entitled

"Rape and other forms of sexual assault."[14] While it reiterates, as might be expected, much of the information available in earlier sources, it also offers some sense of the number of cases for which proof exists that may be used by the United Nations International Criminal Tribunal:

236. The reports contained in the Commission's database identify close to 800 victims by name or number. An additional 1,673 victims are referred to, but not named in reports of victims who indicate that they have witnessed or know of other similar victims. Additionally, there are some 500 reported cases which refer to an unspecified number of victims. The victims' ages, as reported, range from 5 to 81 years old, with the majority of victims below 35 years old. The reported cases identify some 600 alleged perpetrators by name. In other cases, victims refer to a specific number of perpetrators but do not identify them by name. In those cases of unidentified perpetrators, about 900 perpetrators are referred to. Of all the reports received, about 800 contain general information, identifying some perpetrators as soldiers, police, paramilitary, special forces, etc. The alleged perpetrators include military personnel, special forces, local police and civilians. About 80 per cent of the reported cases specify that they occurred in settings where the victims were held in custody.

237. The reported cases of rape and sexual assault contained in the database occurred between the fall of 1991 and the end of 1993. The majority of the rapes occurred from April to November 1992; fewer occurred in the following five months. In the same time period, the number of media reports increased from a few in March 1992 to a high of 535 news stories in January 1993 and 529 in February 1993. This correlation could indicate that the media attention caused the decline. In that case, it would indicate that commanders could con-

trol the alleged perpetrators if they wanted to. This could lead to the conclusion that there was an overriding policy advocating the use of rape as a method of "ethnic cleansing," rather than a policy of omission, tolerating the widespread commission of rape.

After describing five categories of rape as discerned by the commission (see note 7 earlier in this theme), the Bassiouni Report offers the beginnings of an analysis of what it calls "common threads":

250. Common threads run through the cases reported whether within or outside of a detention context:

(*a*) Rapes seem to occur in conjunction with efforts to displace the targeted ethnic group from the region. This may involve heightened shame and humiliation by raping victims in front of adult and minor family members, in front of other detainees or in public places, or by forcing family members to rape each other. Young women and virgins are targeted for rape, along with prominent members of the community and educated women;

(*b*) Many reports state that perpetrators said they were ordered to rape, or that the aim was to ensure that the victims and their families would never want to return to the area. Perpetrators tell female victims that they will bear children of the perpetrator's ethnicity, that they must become pregnant, and then hold them in custody until it is too late for the victims to get an abortion. Victims are threatened that if they ever tell anyone, or anyone discovers what has happened, the perpetrators will hunt them down and kill them;

(*c*) Large groups of perpetrators subject victims to multiple rapes and sexual assault. In detention, perpetrators go through the detention centres with flashlights at night selecting women and return them the next morning, while camp commanders often know about, and sometimes participate in, the sexual assaults;

(*d*) Victims may be sexually abused with foreign objects like broken glass bottles, guns and truncheons. Castrations are performed through crude means such as forcing other internees to bite off a prisoner's testicles.

251. Rape has been reported to have been committed by all sides to the conflict. However, the largest number of reported victims have been Bosnian Muslims, and the largest number of alleged perpetrators have been Bosnian Serbs. There are few reports of rape and sexual assault between members of the same ethnic group.

Torture within Torture

Genocidal rape of non-Serb women by Yugoslav National Army soldiers, Bosnian Serb soldiers, and Serb and Bosnian Serb irregulars occurs not necessarily as a particular torture in preference to all others but most often as a particular torture performed in a context of many other atrocities perpetrated on the same victims and the families, friends, and neighbors of those victims.

In villages, towns, cities, the countryside, and concentration camps, male and female adults and children are raped as part of more extensive torture. Many of the atrocities committed are centered on the genitalia and on the reproductive capacities of the victims. By now, testimonies of castrations enforced on Bosnian-Herzegovinian and Croatian prisoners, and in particular of orders under threat of death that they castrate each other with various instruments and at times with their teeth, are widely available, as the Bassiouni Report makes clear.[15]

Another fact, imparted to me by Dr. Dragica Kozarić-Kovačić, director of the psychiatry department at the distinguished Vrapče Hospital in Zagreb, is that all of the survivors of genocidal rape suffer from multiple trauma—what she calls polytrauma. They have been raped, most of them repeatedly, and have

thus suffered severe genital trauma. They are gravely psychologically traumatized as well. On top of this, many of them need
treatment for severe burns, amputations, and multiple and often
infected incisions. Another common trauma, she said, is the damage done to their throats. They have been strangling for weeks
and months on end as a result of having repeatedly been forced to
swallow vast amounts of urine and sperm.

Amputations are a common form of torture practiced by Serb
and Bosnian Serb military, Chetniks, and other irregular Serb
forces. The most common form of amputation is to cut off the
ring finger and the little finger of the victim's right hand, thus
leaving that hand in an enduring Serb salute (the Orthodox manner of signing the cross is to use three fingers; this salute looks like
a straight-arm Nazi salute with thumb and first two fingers extended; if you look carefully at news photographs of Nazi skin-
heads throughout Europe and the United States, you will find that
many of these young hate mongers have now abandoned the German Nazi salute in favor of the Serb one).[16]

No words can tell the offense to the body when a part of it is
amputated. One form of this particularly horrifying torture has
been reported since 1992 by survivors who witnessed it and who
saw women die from it. This is when the Serb torturers amputate
their Muslim rape victim's breasts and then place her hands in a
cross on her chest, one hand slipped under the flaps of skin that
remain where each breast used to be. In this way the victim is offended symbolically by the mark of her murderer's religion during the last minutes of her life.

The Chetnik Cult of the Knife

Much of the torture is conducted with instruments. These include commonly available objects such as wire, scissors, saws, and other tools used to castrate and amputate body parts. They also include household appliances, such as irons, curling irons, and electrical wiring used to inflict burns and electric shock. By far the most common instrument of torture, however, is the knife.

As the single most important symbol of legendary Serb ultra-nationalist cultism, the knife is also the single most important tool of the pastoral economy in the mountain cultures where such ultranationalism flourishes, the cultures that produced, for example, Radovan Karadžić, leader of the Bosnian Serbs. Bosnian survivors with whom I spoke in Zagreb, women who used to be on the faculties of chemistry and sociology at the University of Sarajevo, remember when he "came down from the mountains," as they put it, to begin his studies in psychology at the university. He was an uncouth bumpkin with offensive manners. During the 1960s, he published a certain amount of poetry. In spite of his provenance in the culture of the knife par excellence, Karadžić himself seems to have been fascinated more with the possibilities of arson than with those of throat slitting, as I mentioned in theme 1.

As an indication of the singular importance of the knife in this cultural cauldron of nationalist madness, we might take another literary endeavor, this time a novel written by Vuk Drašković. Drašković is the leader of a nationalist opposition force within Belgrade; he debuted as a writer in 1982 with a novel entitled *The Knife*.[17] An expurgated translation of this book exists in French, one that leaves out the most terrible massacre scenes (Nahoum-Grappe, 66). The Chetnik cult of the knife is very clear here, where it seems to derive from a pastoral society and the practices of animal butchery.

There is also a film made during the 1970s by the Serb director Mién Popović, and now censored off the market, called *Man from the Woods*; it shows the Chetnik ritual of throat slitting that has been repeated thousands and thousands of times during this genocide (ibid.). Because of its revealing representation of the actual methods being used today, therefore, the film may be considered harmful to the image of the Belgrade government, with whom, after all, well-meaning people are engaged in ongoing negotiations.[18]

The ritual is this: The murderer binds the victim's hands behind her or his back and forces the victim to kneel on the ground. The murderer then jabs his knee into the center of the victim's back, grabs the top of the victim's head by the hair, pulls the victim's head back, and slits the victim's throat with his knife. Over and over again this same macabre posturing spells out death for the civilian population in Bosnia-Herzegovina and Croatia. Many survivors have recounted witnessing just such obsessionally repetitive slaughter.[19]

The knife fixation that seems to characterize both the legendary Serb dream of a Great Serbia reaching to the Austrian border and the official Serb military policy in Bosnia-Herzegovina goes beyond individual accounts of torture and death and suggests instead a collective madness that sweeps all before it in a sea of butchery. Civilians are the main victims of this diseased conflagration: peasants, town dwellers, city dwellers, women, men, children. The knives tear into so much that there is scarcely anything left to kill. In Zagreb, the Croatian, Canadian, and U.S. women who work at Kareta report that when the survivors of rape camps began to reach the Croatian capital from the hinterlands of Bosnia-Herzegovina in the spring of 1992, one of them made it very clear: *we have fled not from bombs and bullets but from rape and the knife.*

I will never forget a visit to the Zapruote refugee camp in Zagreb in November 1993. The first snows had just arrived, and the weather was bitterly cold when the publisher Nenad Popović picked me up at the well-known Intercontinental Hotel.[20] Since I had never been to a refugee camp before, he warned me that I would probably be overwhelmed with a desire to help the people I was about to meet. I would want, for example, to take off my warm woolen coat and give it to someone, to give my woolen hat to someone else, my gloves to still another. He said I must not begin this process, that it would end by leaving me impoverished and thus unable to finish the work I had begun. In fact, I have learned that such "help" at an individual level is a very tricky business, both in the giving and in the receiving. It limits aid to what I think the recipients need, and it may offend them as well. Help is, I believe, much more effective when channeled through the groups I have met. Yet I react at a very personal level and understand such reactions in others. These are enigmas I have yet to resolve.

Nenad, in any case, had been right. This "camp" was a bunch of dormitories next to a factory—places where workers from the countryside had formerly been housed under the most spartan conditions. Now those conditions had deteriorated to the point that people were living two or three to a small room. What beds there were generally had no blankets and no sheets. Pathways between buildings had become ruts of mud now mixed with snow, and none of the buildings was heated. I saw elderly women and men, middle-aged and young women, adolescents of both sexes, and many children. Many of them, the elderly women in particular, were walking through the snow in fabric slippers. One young woman walked by holding a tightly wrapped bundle in her hands, clearly a newborn infant.

Nenad and I found our way to a kind of recreation room next to where a French organization, Secours populaire, had set up a classroom. This recreation room, which was no warmer than any other room in this miserable place, contained one item: a ping-pong table. Here the teenage boys were gathered. Most of them had sweaters. One had only a jean jacket. None of them had winter jackets or coats. I thought of the U.S. middle-class rush to sporting-goods stores for down jackets at the first sign of fall. Here a down jacket would save a life. Nenad explained who we were and asked if we could talk with them for a few minutes. When they shook hands with us, I saw that all their fingers were blue from the cold. With what I have learned to identify as typical Bosnian-Herzegovinian hospitality, one of them invited us to his room. Another came along, and the two of them knocked on some doors along the way to invite a couple of teenage girls to join us.

The girls delayed their arrival long enough to prepare themselves for meeting foreigners by putting on the head scarves that function as a kind of veil. Nenad later explained that these teenagers, most of whom had been quite secular before the aggression, and who in all other respects looked like our own children and their friends (who were dressed, that is, in flowered skirts and big sweaters that in California would be considered sort of hippie), had begun to wear the veil out of respect for the fundamentalist Muslim organizations that provided the camp's only ongoing aid. People from these groups had established and were running the school there, for example, although I find such fundamentalism to be atypical of Islam among the Bosnian-Herzegovinians I have met.

Only one of the boys refused to go to school. The others were worried about him. If he stayed away from school for all the time he was going to be in the refugee camp, he would miss his entire high-school education and would be very bad off once they got out. Amid smiles, immense politeness, and a dulcet friendliness that I was amazed to find under the circumstances, he explained that he was just too bitter to study. The others did not criticize him.

We talked about our families. It turns out that all four of the teenagers Nenad and I spoke with were "unaccompanied children," in the parlance of the United Nations High Commission for Refugees. They were without the benefit, that is, of any accompanying relatives with whom they could maintain at least some family structure within the camp, within the maze of waiting, anguish, and attempts at documentation that characterize the lives of refugees.

I asked them where their families were. The boy in the jean jacket told me his mother and father were in Bosnia-Herzegovina and that he had recently learned that his father had lost an arm. Two of the others were orphans. The fourth, a lovely girl who reminded me of some of my son's friends back in California, gently told us that she had learned one week earlier that her father had been killed in Bosnia-Herzegovina about two weeks prior to that. When we left the camp, I commented to Nenad that this death had not been a bullet death, had it, and he shook his head and said no, probably not: the knife.

The Bloody Sheets

Now I shall tell how I lost, in one moment, the last big chunk of resistance that had been keeping me from believing the worst, the very worst. I know this moment has come in different ways to different people. Anyone who takes the trouble to learn what Serb policy has been accomplishing, and how systematically, is bound sooner or later to arrive at such a moment. Sometimes it's just a little thing that gets you there. Sometimes it's enormous. In any case, afterward you are not the same. For me it happened with one particular story about some bloody sheets.

It was Easter 1993, and M. had come to Syracuse to participate in the symposium on genocidal rape organized by the International Law Students' Association at the Syracuse Law School. She was staying at my house, and my son had come up from Swarthmore as well. So there were three of us, cooking and hanging out, going over to Ithaca to visit Cornell University, shopping a little. M. was reading novels for the first time in months in an effort to give herself a break from the horrors she faced in her work. My son was practicing his electric bass and perfecting his culinary talents. We set to work one evening making baklava according to the Bosnian recipe and the coaching M.'s mother was giving us by telephone. It turned out great.

As happens to many concerned people, however, M. could not avoid talking about the war and the atrocities. One evening she mentioned a story she hadn't yet been able to confirm but had heard bits and pieces of from various sources. It seems, she said, that in one rape/death camp within a concentration camp the women were being raped on bloody sheets. This image conjured up for me a whole cultural repertoire of wedding-night lore, images of the one little spot that confirms the bride's purity, tales of how to fake the spot, even operations southern Italian women had still been having in 1970 in order to reconstruct their hymens prior to their wedding night.[21]

Such images flew away as M. went on to say that apparently these sheets were bloody because they were spread over cots and tables that had previously been used during tortures the Serb guards had been performing on the male prisoners, including relatives and friends of the women victims. These tortures included all sorts of amputations, she had heard, from the common one of two fingers to castrations and other even more extensive maimings.

I was jolted out of my own cultural repertoire and into a new realism. Yet my own darkest moment, or what until now has been the darkest, was still to come.

Months later in Zagreb, the story of the bloody sheets came to mind again during a conversation with a member of Kareta. I mentioned that M. had told me this story that was just about the worst thing I had heard, but that she still didn't have a sense whether it was true or not. Ah, yes, the bloody sheets, my Kareta friend replied. It seems there's something a little strange about that story.

Oh, I thought, thank God. So it's not going to be true after all. Human depravity does not go this far. We got it wrong. There's hope.

Yes, something strange, she continued. More and more survivors have been talking about this, but it turns out the sheets weren't sheets at all. No, it turns out that the women were raped on bloody *rags*, rags they had been forced to use each day to mop up the blood and gore in the room where, during the night, the amputations and other tortures had been performed.

For some reason, this particular detail ended whatever was left of my denial. The difference rags made, where before there had been sheets, was enough to sweep me out of my defensive assumptions and bring me to accept the vast moral and ethical void that I now perceived. Not only were things not better than I had hoped, they were far, far worse.

Can we still call this a "war"? Is "genocide" strong enough?

Theme 4

ANALYSIS

Enforced pregnancy as a method of genocide makes sense only if you are ignorant about genetics. No baby born from such a crime will be only Serb. It will receive half its genetic material from its mother. Moreover, it will be raised within the mother's culture—if her culture survives anywhere, that is. The Serb policy of genocidal rape aimed at pregnancy offers the specter that making more babies with a people equals killing that people off. This illogic is possible only because the policy's authors erase all identity characteristics of the mother other than that as a sexual container.

It has been surprisingly difficult for many who are concerned about this phenomenon to recognize the blatant contradiction it contains, even though it is precisely that contradiction that makes this particular atrocity restive to most international war-crime legislation. Even feminists who have experience in gender-aware analysis often fail to note the specific way in which the Serb policy erases the victim's cultural identity and treats her as nothing more than a kind of biological box. As a result of this critical blindness,

such feminist analyses have, by a logic shockingly similar to the
Serb one, also erased all the victims' identities but the sexual.

Susan Brownmiller, whose 1975 study of rape is staunchly en-
sconced in the U.S. feminist theory canon, comes very close to
just this sort of erasure. In an article carried by the *Newsweek* issue of January 4, 1993, that devoted its cover story to "A Pattern
of Rape: War Crimes in Bosnia," Brownmiller, in "Making Female Bodies the Battlefield," hastens to emphasize the crime of
rape as a crime of violence based on the gender relations that pertain in patriarchy, and thus, by her reasoning, one unfortunately
endemic to all wars. She dismisses a TV newscaster's line, "This is
all about identity," for example, by suggesting he should have
amended it to say "*male* identity." She reminds us of the univer-
sality of rape during wartime and callously challenges what she
calls the "emotional Bosnian appeal" that "calls the Serb rapes
'unprecedented in the history of war crimes,' " and "an organized, systematic attempt 'to destroy a whole Muslim population,
to destroy a society's cultural, traditional and religious integrity' "
(37). She laments: "Alas for women, there is nothing unprecedented about mass rape in war when enemy soldiers advance
swiftly through populous regions, nor is it a precedent when,
howling in misery, leaders of the overrun country call the endemic sexual violence a conspiracy to destroy their national pride,
their manhood, their honor" (ibid.).

Brownmiller reminds us of the historically all too common patriarchal association of the female body with territory, so that raping one and conquering the other come metaphorically to the
same thing:[1]

Women are raped in war by ordinary youths as casually, or as fre-

netically, as a village is looted or gratuitously destroyed. Sexual tres-
pass on the enemy's women is one of the satisfactions of conquest,
like a boot in the face, for once he is handed a rifle and told to kill,
the soldier becomes an adrenaline-rushed young man with permission to kick in the door, to grab, to steal, to give vent to his sub-
merged rage against all women *who belong to other men*. (Ibid.; emphasis in the original)

Brownmiller has much of this right. She may well be describing
the crimes of rape perpetrated by Croatians, Bosnian-Herzegovinians, and Unprofor soldiers. But she misses the criminal
specificity of what the Serbs are doing because she leaves out the
role of impregnation in the Serb policy. She gets close when she
notes the lasting effects of such rape, even if not by means of
childbirth and child raising, when she says:

Sexual sadism arises with astonishing rapidity in ground warfare,
when the penis becomes justified as a weapon in a logistical reality
of unarmed noncombatants, encircled and trapped. Rape of a dou-
bly dehumanized object—as woman, as enemy—carries its own
terrible logic. In one act of aggression, the collective spirit of
women *and* of the nation is broken, leaving a reminder long after
the troops depart. And if she survives the assault, what does the victim of wartime rape become to her people? Evidence of the enemy's
bestiality. Symbol of her nation's defeat. A pariah. Damaged property. A pawn in the subtle wars of international propaganda. (Ibid.)

These postwar identities would assume no possible recupera-
tion of survivors by their own cultures. Brownmiller's images thus
contribute to a larger, more generic Western European and U.S.
cant about demonic Muslims rejecting "their" women. Such generic demonization of Muslims as the implicit "people" of her

article sounds almost Serb in its rhetoric. Brownmiller's insistence
on the damaging effects of patriarchy, with which I do not dis-
agree, neglects many recuperative possibilities available in the cultures involved.[2] Brownmiller might be confusing racist clichés of
Middle Eastern Arabs with the southern Slav heirs to the Bogomils. Culture, in her analysis, is reduced to patriarchy alone. According to Brownmiller, rape in war is simply the way it is in patriarchy. Thus the category "patriarchy" becomes global, erasing
significant cultural differences, erasing pockets of resistance, erasing the ways in which patriarchy harms not only females but
males as well.

Her reduction, unfortunately, also erases the victims' identities
when they are male adults, female children, and male children.
Testimony tells us of male victims in countless villages and concentration camps. The Brana Plan establishes the necessity of
attacking Bosnian-Herzegovinian society at its weakest point,
"women and children." To call the victims of genocidal rape
"women" backfires for Brownmiller's analysis. It ignores the fact
that the violent crime of rape can be perpetrated on anyone, re-
gardless of sex. It ignores the degree to which any rape victim
is—by virtue of her or his very victimage—gendered as feminine.
And, worst of all, it naturalizes "women" as victims.

It is true that "there is nothing unprecedented about mass rape
in war," as Brownmiller says. But to assume that the Serb policy
of genocidal rape is but one more instance of "mass rape in war"
is to miss the novelty, the literal newness, of its bent logic. This
"mass rape in war" is the systematic annihilation of another
people by means of rape, death, and pregnancy in a process psy-
chiatrically designed to destroy the entire culture—the people,

their places, their history, their future. Brutal paradox has the upper hand here, and Brownmiller misses it: the *pregnancies*, and not the rapes alone, are a major weapon of the genocide. There may be "nothing unprecedented about mass rape in war," but this is something new.

Think about the legendary rape of the Sabines in the eighth century B.C.E. According to legend, Romulus's conquering troops made off with the Sabine women (thus committing "rape," in the sense of "kidnap," in addition to rape as genital violence) who inhabited the Italic peninsula. After prolonged battles with their husbands, Romulus's troops married those women themselves and made peace with the surviving Sabine men (Cook, Adcock, and Charlesworth; Harvey). Because it depends for its effectiveness on the eventual pregnancies of many of the victims, the rape of the Sabines comes close to resembling Serb genocidal rape. Its purpose, however, was precisely the opposite: to establish new families that eventually formed the Roman population. Because the rapists in this legend married their victims and formed a new culture, the legendary rape of the Sabines is no precedent for the present-day genocidal practice of the Serbs.

Think about the horrors of the Shoah, when the Nazis distinguished themselves in the annals of evil by turning modernity on its ear. Scientific methodology and even medical procedures became instruments of torture used on persons who had been so successfully demonized and dehumanized that no vestige of ethical or moral hesitation remained in the torturers. Yet not even the Nazis managed to invent a way to turn the biological process of gestation into a weapon of annihilation. In fact, it is impossible to think that any Nazi rapist knowingly would have agreed to propagate with a Jewess. Genocidal rape aimed at enforced pregnancy would seem to be a peculiarly Serb contribution to the history of atrocity.[3]

In the end, therefore, Brownmiller's analysis misses the single most significant characteristic, the historically new trait, of the current Serb genocidal rape policy: as *impregnation*, it is genocide. This is precisely its logical glitch. Brownmiller thus leaves unanswered the evident question: how can rape, forced pregnancy, and resultant childbirths, the production of new persons, be genocide, the annihilation of a people?

The Croatian writer Slavenka Drakulić comes closer to answering this question in an article published in the *Nation* (March 1, 1993). Entitled "Women behind a Wall of Silence," this piece describes a visit Drakulić makes to the refugee camp at Resnik, near Zagreb, where she presses unsuccessfully to get some Bosnian-Herzegovinian women to speak about what she assumes must have been their experiences in rape/death camps. With almost no exceptions, the women remain silent, or at most they recount atrocities as if they had been performed on someone else.[4] Drakulić takes this as normal, given the gender politics of the Muslim communities in Bosnia-Herzegovina. She misses the degree to which Catholic or Orthodox women might also hesitate to speak with a stranger about atrocities that dishonor them and that they would rather forget. Drakulić views Bosnian-Herzegovinian society as entirely Muslim and therefore patriarchal, as if Catholic or Orthodox cultures were by definition otherwise. She thus erases all Bosnian-Herzegovinian cultures other than the Muslim one at the same time that she curiously underestimates the power of the very patriarchy she condemns.

Although she equates patriarchy solely with Islam, instead of limiting her blame for the women's silence to that patriarchy, Drakulić actually goes on to blame the women themselves. She implies that these survivors, who now must face the rigors and grave uncertainties of refugee life, should somehow simply overcome what she considers to be their unnecessary hesitancy and offer their testimony, first for her satisfaction and her article, and then for use at a war crimes tribunal. She thereby engages in the worst kind of blaming the victim—because it is indirect and implicit—in reading their "silence" as a survival strategy that they should relinquish within their (implicitly uniquely) oppressive Muslim community. It never occurs to her that this silence might be a refusal to speak these things to Drakulić herself, that she might be for them an intruding stranger who will use their words for her own ends. She writes:

> When Mersiha talked, the other women didn't comment. They stared at the floor as if they were guilty, as if they were to blame. I asked Mersiha, But what about you? She looked at her mother, sitting there and listening, as if asking her for permission to say more. "No, it did not happen to me," she said, but I doubted her. Maybe, if I came on another day, she would decide to tell her *true* story. That is how it works; only patience and empathy can break the wall of self-protection. (270; emphasis mine)

How does Drakulić know Mersiha's true story if Mersiha does not tell it? What right does she have to "break the wall of self-protection" Mersiha so clearly needs? Drakulić is making assumptions, conjuring up a rape narrative that she already has in mind, chiding Mersiha for keeping it from her avid ears. She thus denies Mersiha the right to keep herself as safe as possible from the invasion Drakulić's interrogation adds to whatever pain has already been inflicted.

A very different approach to refugee women who may well be survivors of genocidal rape is taken by the psychiatrist Dr. Narcisa Sarajlić of the Ruke group in Zagreb. Dr. Sarajlić and her group make weekly visits to the same camp, Resnik, where Drakulić met Mersiha. The refugees in Resnik feel very close to this camp, Dr. Sarajlić says, because they organized it themselves. Dr. Sarajlić sometimes asks refugees about their traumatic experiences, but she never prods them to speak. Sometimes they do so immediately, as if it were nothing. Most often, however, they try to repress it. Dr. Sarajlić has two young female patients in Resnik who are survivors of rape/death camps. It took them over a year and a half of regular psychotherapeutic sessions with her before they felt safe enough to mention the rapes they had suffered.

Tadeusz Mazowiecki and his team of investigators have found this sort of caution and witness fatigue among survivors of genocidal rape. In their June 30, 1993, report, for example, they note that the consequences of insensitive attempts to gather testimony can be disastrous:

13. Regarding the gathering of testimony from rape victims, the Special Rapporteur pointed out in his February report that many women are reluctant to speak about their experiences for a variety of reasons: severe traumatization, feelings of shame, lack of trust, fear of awakening bad memories as well as fear of reprisals against themselves and their families. Repeated interviewing of victims by a number of missions and some media representatives has further decreased their readiness to testify. Some of the women met by the team of experts felt exploited by the media and the many missions "studying" rape in the former Yugoslavia. Furthermore, health care

providers are concerned about the effects on women of repeatedly recounting their experiences without adequate psychological and social support systems in place. The danger of subjecting women to additional emotional hardship in the course of interviews is a real one. There have been reports of women attempting suicide after being interviewed by the media and well-meaning delegations. (United Nations Economic and Social Council, 5)

Given this reality, it is hard to imagine that survivors would easily speak of such things with Drakulić, who is neither an official investigator nor just any ordinary journalist, but an internationally known, and controversial, writer.[5] For all the opposition to Drakulić from both Bosnian-Herzegovinian and Croatian women in Zagreb, and in spite of her opportunistic behavior even with persons who might be survivors of genocidal rape, she at least comes closer to understanding the paradox of the Serb equation—that rape, enforced pregnancy, and enforced childbirth equal genocide—than does Brownmiller. Drakulić writes:

What seems to be unprecedented about the rapes of Muslim women in Bosnia (and, to a lesser extent, the Croat women too) is that there is a clear *political* purpose behind the practice. The rapes in Bosnia are not only a standard tactic of war, they are an organized and systematic attempt to cleanse (to move, resettle, exile) the Muslim population from certain territories Serbs want to conquer in order to establish a Greater Serbia. (Drakulić, 271)

Drakulić has taken the trouble to learn something about genocidal rape, which she views as the female counterpart of the extermination of males that happens in the Serb camps:

The eyewitness accounts and reports state that women are raped everywhere and at all times, and victims are of all ages, from 6 to 80. They are also deliberately impregnated in great numbers (the Bosnian government estimates that some 35,000 of them have been impregnated, unbelievable as it may sound), held captive and released only after abortion becomes impossible. This is so they will "give birth to little Chetniks," the women are told. While Muslim men are killed fighting or are exterminated in about 100 concentration camps (the Bosnian government estimates that as many as 120,000 people have been killed or have died in the Bosnian war up to now and some 60,000 are missing, while the U.S. State Department estimate for those killed is as low as 17,000), women are raped and impregnated and expelled from their country. *Thus not only is their cultural and religious integrity destroyed but the reproductive potential of the whole nation is threatened.* (Ibid.; emphasis mine)

This is where Drakulić slips up. The genocidal logic of rape for impregnation is not only that it threatens the targeted people's reproductive potential. Any mass killings threaten reproduction by limiting the number of reproducers. Any rape threatens reproduction because it makes survivors damaged goods in a patriarchal system that defines woman as man's possession and virgin woman as his most valuable asset.

The particularity of the current Serb genocidal policy of rape for impregnation lies instead precisely in its logical glitch. The Chetnik or Serb soldier who, while raping, believes he is creating "little Chetniks" or "Serb soldier-heroes" is, in fact, mistaken according to every relevant identity context, from the most specifically scientific to the most specifically cultural. Speaking in strictly genetic terms, for example, if his sperm does fertilize an egg, the resultant zygote will contain an equal amount of genetic material from its non-Chetnik, non-Serb mother as it will from its Chetnik or Serb father. Biology thus gives the lie to the Serb military policy.

Culture (though I do not mean to consider this as entirely separate from biology) does the same thing. Any child produced by such forced impregnation, unless that child is raised by its Serb father in a Serb community, will be assimilated to the cultural, ethnic, religious, national identity of the mother. To call such children "Chetniks" or "little Serb soldiers" is clearly a blatant, though highly motivated, stupidity. Serb "ethnic cleansing" by means of rape, enforced pregnancy, and childbirth is based on the uninformed, hallucinatory fantasy of ultranationalists whose most salient characteristic, after their violence, is their ignorance.

Finally, in terms of sex, and this is perhaps its greatest signifi cance, the Serb policy equation whereby impregnation by rape equals genocide depends entirely on the rapists' capacity to deny any identity of their victims other than that as a sexual container. Here is genocidal rape's most bizarre paradox: if the Serbs want their formula to work, it must be implemented with persons whose ethnic, religious, or national identities have been erased. It must be performed on women who have, for purposes of the Serb father equals Serb baby equation, no identity beyond sex—on women, that is, who in theory *no longer bear the marks of ethnicity, religion, or nationality that the Serb military and the Bosnian Serbs used to justify their aggression in the first place.*

Whether most of the perpetrators see this erasure is a question I cannot answer. Survivors report that some Serbs have initially refused to rape and have been severely punished and even killed for this. Survivors have also testified that some Serbs are physically incapable of performing the rapes on order. To guard against such a shortcoming, they make use of pornographic material and drugs that evidently help to short-circuit whatever moral and ethical resistance they may have and to induce the psychological and physical states necessary for rape. Reports of mass drunkenness among the perpetrators also exist, although one would think that drunkenness, while it might remove any vestigial psychological inhibitions against committing atrocities, would in fact inhibit the physical erections on which so much genocide now depends.[6]

Other means are used to psych up the perpetrators. Survivors attest to the rapists' use of ethnic-based expletives (such as "ustasha") as well as sex-based ones ("bitch," "whore," and so forth).[7] It would seem from the ethnic- and sex-based expletives in particular that the perpetrators are raping because the women are Muslim or Catholics just as much as because they are women. The policy of genocidal rape, nonetheless, is founded upon the illogical reasoning that procreation of Muslim-Serb or Catholic-Serb offspring equals the destruction of the Bosnian-Herzegovinian or Croatian populations and the purification of the Serb one. This is perfectly in keeping with the notion—one that permeates Serb ultranationalist legend, literature, and propaganda—that wherever a Serb is buried, there lies Serb territory.[8]

One of the most tragic psychological results of this policy is that the victims, if they survive, often do so believing the Serb illogic. Quite in spite of themselves, they may finally, at some level, begin to subscribe to the very reasoning that erases their cultural identity. They are expelled from the camps convinced at least to some degree that the pregnancy they carry will result in the birth of a Chetnik, a Serb, a child who will have none of her or his mother's characteristics. This conviction, the result of continuous psychological torture in the context of other seemingly limitless physical torture, leads many survivors to attempt third-trimester abortions or to commit suicide. Barring that, many attempt to kill their babies at birth in a reaction that, speaking strictly in terms of the mother's psychological well-being, might even be considered healthy. Psychiatrists in Zagreb remind me that such a reaction is not necessarily due to the mother's fear of shame within her own community. It derives more often from the mother's conviction that her offspring, quite simply, is the enemy. At some level, she hates it and wants to destroy it. It is part of what has so dreadfully destroyed her town, harmed her, tortured, maimed, and slit the throats of her loved ones.

Dr. Kozarić-Kovačić tells me that another common reaction on the part of the mothers, especially those who are thirteen, fourteen, fifteen years old, is an altruistic one. They fear that, because of what they have suffered from the baby's father, they will never be able to give this child the love and tenderness that the baby, an innocent being, deserves. If they survive their impulse to suicide and manage to give birth, such survivors often quite simply get up from their ward beds when no one is looking and walk out the hospital door. They leave the infant to less traumatized caregivers, even though this means breaking contact with those caregivers themselves, never returning to Dr. Kozarić-Kovačić or other caregivers, and abandoning themselves to the shadow world of refugee life, now often quite alone.

Finally, although not enough has been said in the U.S. and Western European media about Serb genocidal rape, relatively great attention has been given to the reactions or supposed reactions of the survivors' communities. According to some people (including Slavenka Drakulić) who have spoken with survivors, many of them feel cast away by their own communities. As I said earlier, this is a very partial picture. In fact, there is often no community reaction and no family reaction whatsoever because there is quite simply no more community and no more family to react. The towns have been destroyed. The families have been slaughtered. The rape survivors are "going back" to nowhere. At the very best, they'll get to a refugee camp in Germany, perhaps. Bosnian-Herzegovinian and Croatian refugees may soon be spread all over the world. Although it is clear that patriarchal societies devalue women who have been victims of rape, some of the rejecting "communities" that haunt the guilty, parsimonious international coverage of genocidal rape may be, quite literally, inexistent.

In summary, the specific characteristics that mark the Serb policy of genocidal rape are the following:

1. It is aimed at the destruction of a people.
2. It determines that this aim will best be served by attacking women and children in particular.
3. It considers the violent crime of rape to be an ideal means to this destruction.
4. It utilizes rape as one form of torture preceding death; in this case, rape is used against male and female adults and male and female children.
5. It utilizes rape as a means of enforcing pregnancy and eventual childbirth; in this case, rape is used against persons capable of gestating a pregnancy.
6. In the case of enforced pregnancy, its illogical reasoning is founded on the negation of all cultural identities of its victims, reducing those victims to mere sexual containers.
7. Although it may occur anywhere, it generally occurs in three locales:

(*a*) towns and villages, where it is often performed
    publicly, most often on female women and children;

(*b*) concentration camps, where it is generally performed
    sporadically on prisoners regardless of age or sex;

(*c*) rape/death camps, where it is performed systematically
    on female women and children (note that rape/death
    camps exist sometimes within concentration camps).

Genocidal rape aimed at enforced pregnancy and eventual
childbirth, therefore, erases the cultural identity of the victim, the
very characteristics that ostensibly made that person an enemy in
the first place. Once these are erased, however, the victim still remains an enemy; that is, even when she has been reduced in the
logic of the Brana Plan to a mere sexual container, she must still
be destroyed. Therefore, in this aggression, the novelty of the
Brana Plan for genocidal rape aimed at enforced pregnancy is
this: in the final analysis, after the sick logic of genocidal rape has
canceled her cultural identity, the victim still qualifies as an enemy because of her sex alone. This life-and-death choreography
of cultural and biological identity is precisely what is at stake in
any legal recourse the victims may have.

Theme 5

REMEDIES

History and Politics: A Note

As I write about these things, I am reminded over and over again of the angel of history Walter Benjamin imagines in his "Theses on the Philosophy of History" (75-86). Flying backward into the future, the gape-mouthed angel sees the wreckage of the past grow ever more vast in its wake. What would the angel remake in this heap in order to guarantee peace in the future it rushes into but cannot see? Benjamin's angel shows the tragic futility of hindsight, which, alas, is the only sight it has.

To speak of political or military remedies in 1995 is to engage the angel's vision. Had the victors of World War II partitioned Eastern Europe differently; had Tito's succession worked successful Yugoslav solutions to an era when the superpowers were reduced from two to one; had there been any democratic institutions in the southern Slav republics; had the pogroms within the Yugoslav National Army been stopped; had the world better understood the political (and not racist) nature of Slovenian, Croatian, and Bosnian-Herzegovinian independence; had the Bosnian-

Herzegovinians been armed to the same degree as the Serbs and the Bosnian Serbs; had Clinton maintained his campaign promise to intervene militarily in 1993; had European countries intervened to prevent this second twentieth-century genocide in Europe; had NATO acted according to the spirit its existence implies; had the United Nations done what its charter says it should, the Serb aggression into Slovenia, Croatia, and Bosnia-Herzegovina and the Bosnian Serb aggression within Croatia and Bosnia-Herzegovina might not have happened and the genocide might have been stopped. Effectively, however, no one did anything to check the firestorm of Serb ultranationalism. In fact, except for its initial defeat in Slovenia, the Serb territorial aggression has been a model of success. The Yugoslav Army and the Bosnian Serb forces now occupy a vast majority of the territory of Bosnia-Herzegovina. Furthermore, the Serb genocide of non-Serbs has been so successful that not only has it massacred hundreds of thousands of people and permanently maimed or traumatized hundreds of thousands more (including the children borne by the thousands of adolescent and adult females forcibly impregnated by genocidal rape), not only has it wiped hundreds of Bosnian-Herzegovinian and Croatian towns, villages, and cities off the face of the globe, producing hundreds of thousands of permanent refugees and displaced persons; it has also served as a model of behavior for Croat and even Bosnian-Herzegovinian forces to imitate at times. The moral degradation of this amoebic spread of atrocity thus infects the social fiber of the cultures most victimized by it to begin with.

I am too full of nausea at the lack of response by the U.S. government to elaborate on the fact that I met and admired Warren Christopher when he was on the Board of Trustees at Stanford

University, where I taught for eight years. I am sad beyond words that some of my own friends in California talk about how they cannot bring themselves to agree to send their own sons, those boys who, though professional soldiers if they are in the armed forces, are different from all others because they are *American*, to fight (for principles upon which American democracy is based, but no one mentions this) in such a messy war where of course the terrain is as convoluted as the tribal peoples' mentality, and for what—to side with one bloodthirsty tribe against others of the same ilk? Where were these delicate objections when George Bush produced the Gulf War? The invasion of Nicaragua? It seems as if wars of aggression are entirely acceptable, particularly because the United States engages in them, and genocide is the rule of the day, whether the Serbs do it in Bosnia-Herzegovina and Croatia, or the immigration authorities do it on the Mexican border or the sea routes from Haiti, or the inhabitants of Rwanda do it to each other. Not all the Yankee tongue-clucking of the second half of this century can drown out the human suffering that U.S. foreign policy allows in spite of all its well-intended or calculated rhetoric to the contrary.

I shall not, therefore, discuss military solutions here except to say that it has long been evident to me that, at the very least, the arms embargo should be lifted so that the army of Bosnia-Herzegovina can defend itself and fight to regain territory conquered by the criminal Serb aggression. I shall not, furthermore, discuss so-called political solutions. These are a priori not solutions, since they depend on negotiations with the architects and top producers of the most blatant international aggression and the most atrocious war crimes in Europe since Hitler's Nazis. Any political agreements, therefore, are by definition not trustworthy or just. I believe that the war will continue for a long time. Were Western Europe and the United States to take decisive military action now, some injustice could be righted and much suffering could be avoided. In the meanwhile, I react to their current policies with a politics of my own, what the Italian poet Zanzotto calls "the politics of continuous vomiting" (111).

Humanitarian Remedies

No one I have met in Zagreb, whether they were from Sarajevo or Karlovac or anywhere else, has said that there should be no humanitarian aid. Just about everyone, however, complains that the aim of such aid, particularly when it is organized on a mass scale, is liable to be severely perverted. UN convoys, for example, are easily ambushed, and their contents often end up on the black market. Serb roadblocks have plagued relief efforts since they began. One I heard about refused to let a UN convoy pass into Bosnia-Herzegovina because the Serbs claimed to have found material for building bombs on board the trucks. These "bomb components" were simply rolls of plastic sheeting for displaced persons and refugees to use in building winter shelters.

Particular bitterness comes from the Sarajevans I've met, who, though not the only victims of Serb sieges, have been the most visible. If they have stayed alive, this is due in great part to international humanitarian aid; they realize this with the clarity of the damned. But this "humanitarian" aid has been accompanied by the almost total refusal of the outside world that is providing it to intervene in any way to stop the daily slaughter of Sarajevans who the UN powdered milk was keeping alive. A Sarajevan chemist at Bišer told me that sending humanitarian aid to Sarajevo with no military intervention was like sending Spam to Auschwitz.

All intervention is somehow helpful, even when it testifies to the bad conscience and moral cynicism of the official cultures that ratify it. Official organizations intervene awkwardly at best. Some of the most effective remedial work has been done by non-state groups outside Bosnia-Herzegovina and Croatia. I'm thinking, for example, of a grassroots group of concerned people in Turin who to date have brought about three hundred survivors to live and work in Italy. (Among these is the Muslim family mentioned earlier that has decided to raise the baby produced by genocidal rape as their own.) The members of this group are middle-class people with jobs of one sort or another who simply joined forces and began to work. Some of them are attorneys, and the group pays special attention to making sure all the refugees' papers are in order, a very important detail in the life of a survivor.

I could also mention a man in Venice who, upon learning from me something more about the genocide than he had understood from the Italian media, decided to do something himself. Because he owns a moving and storage company, he was ready with a whole fleet of transport boats to collect warm clothing from the citizens of Venice. To this store he added sizable quantities of new shoes, cheeses, salamis, and wine at his own expense. When he had enough to fill a two-ton truck, he and one of his daughters drove these supplies to Zagreb, where they distributed them in a refugee camp with the help of the women of Kareta.

One person can help. Better still, a group of people can help. You can form one. You don't have to be a big organization in order to do something. And it isn't hard to figure out what to do. Call the United Nations, call the Red Cross, call the Red Crescent, call Caritas. Send money to groups listed in the Appendix to this book. *Send money in particular to the women's organizations in Zagreb listed in the Appendix.* These are grassroots groups of Bosnian-Herzegovinian and Croatian women who work directly with survivors of genocidal rape and with all refugees and displaced persons. They have twenty-four-hour hotlines for victims; they have outfitted mobile gynecology and dental clinics (gynecological and dental health care services are not provided in the camps) to visit the refugee camps; they help refugees living with no money in crowded apartments; they provide psychotherapy when it is wanted; they maintain community houses in Zagreb where women can engage in traditional activities and feel less isolated than in refugee apartments; they facilitate contact between family members; they help pregnant survivors; one helps families of journalists murdered during the war (according to the Serb practice of making no distinction between combatants and noncombatants, more journalists have been killed in this war than in all the wars since World War II). *And send money to the No Peace Without Justice campaign.* This is the sole transnational effort aimed at establishing a *permanent* International War Crimes Tribunal. Such a body would provide at least some guarantee that genocidal rape and other war crimes and crimes against humanity, wherever and whenever they occur, would not go unnoticed or unpunished. Furthermore, solving whatever difficulties such a permanent tribunal encounters will go far toward discerning the new forms of authority and jurisdiction that we shall all soon be needing as nation-state forms of government evolve during the coming century.

Legal Remedies

If Benjamin's angel of history has any chance of shaping the future, it may well be through legal or juridical actions taken in regard to military aggression and war crimes. My own concern in this regard is with existing international law, which I will discuss in a moment. Meanwhile, I want to mention an interesting possibility that exists in several countries for bringing the perpetrators of atrocity to judgment, if not justice, and thus (1) limiting their capacity to perpetrate further crimes and (2) limiting their capacity to function as statesmen.

Two traditions of jurisprudence exist in Europe. One, from which the United States' legal system is derived, is the British tradition of common law. Based on practice and precedent and not on a written code, this tradition has one feature that, for the purposes I care about here, is particularly salient: according to the practice of common law, no person can be tried *in contumacia*—that is, without being present for trial.

Since the United Nations International Criminal Tribunal for the former Yugoslavia is designed on the basis of the common law tradition, it can bring to trial only those accused persons who are in the custody of the court. This means that, as regards the untold instances of genocidal rape as well as of other atrocious war crimes, the UN tribunal cannot try the authors of the policy of genocide, genocidal rape, and other war crimes and crimes against humanity, just as it cannot try the commanders of the perpetrating forces who, accepting individual responsibility for war crimes committed in the name of their countries according to a convention all of them signed in London in 1992, will not likely accept any invitation of the tribunal to visit The Hague to be judged. The only persons the tribunal will be able to judge are those individual perpetrators who have been captured. So far, three Serb soldiers stand accused of "rape" (genocidal rape is not officially a crime) and are awaiting trial in a prison in The Hague.[1] One of them was identified by one of his victims in a refugee camp in Germany, where he had taken the identity of another of his victims.

Antonio Cassese, the president of the UN tribunal, recognizes the handicapping effect this aspect of the common law tradition (which of course protects the civil rights of the accused and is a partial guarantor of democratic proceedings) will have on the tribunal's ability to prosecute.[2] Having anticipated this, and in an effort to prosecute effectively such authors of the genocide as may be identified, the judges of the UN tribunal will most likely call upon the UN Security Council to produce those persons accused of war crimes who have not been arrested already, even when such persons are leaders of the parties to the conflict. If the Security Council cooperates, then it will call in turn upon Interpol to arrest these accused war criminals. Although it is unlikely that any persons so identified will facilitate the work of the International Police, international warrants for their arrest would severely hamper their ability to travel and thus to participate in international negotiations, command armed forces, and govern civilian populations.

A tradition of jurisprudence other than that of common law exists in Europe, one derived from Roman Law and modified by Napoleon's massive code. Prevalent in Mediterranean countries, this tradition does permit trial *in contumacia*. In Italy, for example, this aspect of the juridical system combines with one other particularity to make jurisdiction over Serb and other war criminals theoretically possible within the Italian nation-state. That other particularity is a legal instrument that adopts as national law all international conventions and protocols to which the state of Italy is a signatory. Since, therefore, rape and genocide are not only against international law but also, by virtue of this instrument, against Italian law, those accused of these crimes may in fact be brought to trial in an Italian court even though they are not present.

These particularities of national juridical systems that derive from Roman Law and the Napoleonic Code make it possible, theoretically as well as practically, to bring such blatant war criminals as Radovan Karadžić and the Serb army officers who authored the Ram and Brana plans to trial even if they are not present. One such project has already made headway in France, where in May 1994 a judge to whom a case against Serb war criminals had been presented declared himself legally competent to hear it. I know of one group of feminists in Italy who are preparing a similar case, this time specifically against the authors of genocidal rape policy as such, within the Italian juridical system.[3]

In any case, it is imperative that a permanent tribunal be established so that instances of genocidal rape in particular and genocide in general, as well as all other war crimes, may be adjudicated on an ongoing basis. The shifting order of power in the world clearly necessitates this, as I discuss in the final theme of this book.

The Chivalric Remedies of International Law

Given the current institutionalization of transnational society in nation-state-based, international organizations, I have been reading the body of international conventions and protocols that are devised by such institutions and that may be used as the basis of any legal redress for the atrocities I have studied. In particular, I have been looking at international law against genocide, war crimes, and the abuses of human rights in order to determine whether any adequate description of genocidal rape, and in particular of the type of genocidal rape aimed at enforced pregnancy and childbirth, exists. I understand that perpetrators, including those in charge of the Bosnian Serb and Yugoslav National Army personnel who have been ordered to rape for purposes of genocide, and including also the commanding officers of the Yugoslav National Army who wrote the policy of genocidal rape, are liable to prosecution for rape because (1) rape is defined as a war crime in existing conventions and protocols and (2) the leaders of each party to the conflict signed a treaty in London in 1992 accepting individual responsibility for war crimes committed by forces under their command. For purely practical purposes at this time, therefore, my investigation is perhaps unnecessary. For theoretical purposes, however—for purposes, that is, of conceptualizing the crime correctly in order to provide adequate descriptions and appropriate redress in the future—my investigation is not only necessary but urgent. If the historic novelty of this illogical and brutal form of genocide goes undescribed and unrecognized, then female persons the world over will be liable to have their very bodies treated as weapons by aggressors intent on annihilating their communities. Furthermore, the door will be open at a theoretical *and legal* level for war crimes based not only on genetic logic, however faulty, *but also on genetic engineering.* It is therefore imperative that not only all concerned persons, whether they consider themselves feminists or not, but also every single international jurist, and particularly the judges convened to serve as the United Nations International Criminal Tribunal, be apprised of the inadequacy of almost every current definition of war crimes to cover the criminal specificity of the Serb policy of genocidal rape.

Unlike national, state, county, or municipal laws in the United States, which are determined legislatively, the conventions and protocols that compose international law are documents whose binding force is established and agreed to by the signatory parties, which are in all cases nation-states. I have been amazed at the looseness of the weblike structure these documents imply. As I delve into the relatively sparse volumes, I marvel at how law in general is so much about usage, custom, precedent. The law is immensely weighted in favor of the status quo, at least in this almost diaphanous net of international conventions against war crimes and in support of human rights.

I approach these texts with my own tools, those of a literary analyst, the interpreter, the scholar of culture, the attentive reader, the feminist. These encounters with texts are what bind literary and legal scholarship in the first place: we are all after every possible meaning we can find. I note that several basic concepts come into play in this body of work. One of these is the notion that there can be crimes in war in the first place. This notion, which clearly implies that there is a right way and a wrong way to engage in armed conflict (which, after all, implies the distinct possibility that a state may legitimately kill, maim, or otherwise severely harm persons it identifies as the enemy), derives historically, at least in modern times, from medieval codes of chivalry. Killing in war is the delegation to common soldiers of the extreme power claimed by the state: the power to kill with impunity. Killing in war is thus permitted and even desirable from the point of view of the state, even though, with the advent of modern technology, it has become a much more common consequence of battle than it was, say, in the European Middle Ages. Killing in war, however, has vastly divergent meanings depending on how it is accomplished. One of the main things at stake, in the final analysis, is male honor, with all its attendant attributes of power, property, and privilege. Chivalric conventions of warfare, therefore, work to preserve and increase such gendered specificity. All subsequent conventions related to the governance of warfare in Europe and Europe-derived cultures belong to this tradition, which regulates blood frenzy (traditionally engaged in only by males) in order to produce meaning—or a culture—in which male hierarchies as determined in combat (as well as by birth) provide the dominant social structure.

As anyone who has studied chivalric poetry knows, another aspect of the chivalric code is a knight's adoration and protection of (certain) women (aristocrats who are married to someone other than the suitor). This has given rise not only to modern notions of romantic heterosexual love but also to modern notions of romantic heterosexual warfare, where the gender division of labor is acute.[4] The soldier, by definition male, is duty-bound to fight honorably (as defined by international conventions and protocols against war crimes) only against others of similar civic and gender status.

With the advent of the nation-state, and in particular with the development of twentieth-century technologies of warfare, normative modes of warfare deriving from chivalric notions of honorable ways of fighting have been articulated in various international legal instruments. From the Fourth Hague Convention of 1907 on, for example, conventions exist that apply specifically to international conflict and provide the normative base for the war crimes prosecutions that followed the Second World War. These modes legitimate prosecution for what they call grave breaches of the normative (that is, masculinist, honor-based) conduct of war. What is at stake in these early conventions, therefore, is still a feudal notion of male honor, adapted to certain modern-day nation-state exigencies. In these agreements, the nation-state functions as a heterosexual male individual honor-bound within a feudal patriarchy. In theory, all that has changed is the player—from single knight to multitudinous state; the code remains much the same.

War crimes as such, for example, are established in the post-World War II Nuremberg Charter as violations of laws and customs of war by soldiers or by civilians. The Fourth Geneva Convention of 1949 defines such violations, or grave breaches of custom, to include willful murders, torture, inhuman treatment, the willful causing of grave suffering or harm to one's body or one's health, illegal deportation, illegal confinement, and the like (article 147).

In recent decades, however, international law begins to pass from definitions of "war crimes" to definitions of "crimes against humanity," where the normative basis is implicitly no longer a chivalric behavior in battle but a universal notion of human rights. At this point, I begin reading an entirely new literature: international human rights law.

By definition, the sole characteristic an individual would need to display in order to qualify for coverage by such law is the characteristic of being human. Alas, it doesn't quite work that way. Even the best, most useful documents related to the human rights of women often inadvertently reinforce our second-class status as a "special" category of human since we, along with several other "special" kinds of humans, are in need of "special" protection.[5]

One of the recurrent paradoxes of human rights law specifically aimed at protecting women is that such law both provides practical recourse for grave sex-based violations of human rights and reinforces the notion that women, because they have need of such recourse (which, of course, in a practical sense we sometimes do, given the way the system of what's "natural" is tilted against us), *are* a "special" category of human, a kind other than the kind who get to write the enlightened law and do the required protecting in the first place. An example of this is the (practically very valuable) United Nations Human Rights Document HRI/GEN/1 of September 4, 1992, on the elimination of discrimination against women. On the one hand, this instrument clearly defines some of the gravest modes of sex- and gender-based oppression that female persons suffer on a global scale. It includes not only rape but also such other seriously harmful realities as the traditional stereotyping of women as objects of submission, pornography depicting women as sexual objects rather than as respectable human beings, and thus encouraging sexual violence, trafficking in women, sexual tourism, recruitment of domestic workers in developing countries to work in developed countries, sexual harassment in the workplace, traditional relegation of women in rural areas to subaltern positions, forced sterilization and abortion, and domestic violence (76-79). On the other hand, it defines these sex- and gender-based crimes simply as forms of *discrimination*. The report begins: "1. Sex-based violence is a form of *discrimination* that seriously prevents women from enjoying rights and liberties to the same extent as men do" (76) (my translation from the French; emphasis mine).

Gender, as represented by the use of the word "women," is a trap here. In human rights law, "human" is theoretically a universal biological condition, which, whatever its variant appearances, is not determined by culture. "Woman," on the other hand, is a cultural definition par excellence; its meaning varies considerably from one society to another, and even within a given society. It lends itself to varied definitions based, for example, on age, so-called race, class, virginity, fecundity, and maternity. International human rights instruments, therefore, contain at their core a contradiction that undermines the foundational principle on which they are based: any mention they make of "women" utilizes a cultural definition, whereas human rights by definition transcend culture. This contradiction allows for the paradox of special categories of humans (humans who are somehow less than real ones) to be protected by the real ones (by definition male) in a pattern that reproduces, centuries later, the late-medieval chivalric code that in the modern era helped to get the regulation of warfare going in the first place.[6]

Ungendering (Deculturating) Rape

As a culturally determined category, "woman" is also a gender, rather than a sex, definition. I think of it this way: Gender is a cultural determination of identity, behavior, appearance, or endeavor as feminine or masculine. Sexuality is a cultural definition given to the workings of desire as determined by the gender identity of both the subject and the object. (If I am a female and I desire a male, I am heterosexual; if I am a female and I desire a female, I am homosexual, and so on.) Sex is the biological definition given to combinations of physical characteristics occurring at birth or appearing during one's lifetime. Sex occurs across a gamut from female to male; it may be discerned in five naturally occurring sexes, two of which are vastly predominant (female and male), three of which are hermaphroditic (herms, merms, and ferms), in varied proportions of female and male characteristics, and none of which lends itself to hard-and-fast characterization. All of these definitions are provisional and matters of ongoing discussion.

Some movement away from normative (male-based, chivalric-encoded, and paradoxically exclusive) gendered definitions of rape is detectable in recent UN human rights instruments. In particular, the work of Mazowiecki and his group has made progress away from both gendered (and thus culturally variable) definitions and definitions that declare rape to be (implicitly merely) a form of discrimination. One may assume that earlier definitions of rape as discrimination were oriented toward the practical need to include rape and other forms of violence practiced mostly against females as punishable crimes under preexisting international protocols condemning discrimination as such. Such a practical exigency, however helpful and desirable it may be on a short-term basis, opens the way for severe theoretical difficulties that are bound to hinder more equitable legal recourse in the long run. Fortunately, Mazowiecki, clearly spurred by what he has witnessed in Bosnia-Herzegovina and Croatia, has provided a definition of rape that satisfies several urgent theoretical (and now, with the tribunal, practical) needs: (1) it defines rape as a crime of violence; (2) it defines rape in ungendered terms—that is, it does not naturalize women as rape's victims nor does it depend on a cultural definition of women; (3) it clarifies the dynamic of power and subjugation attendant to rape, thus making it difficult to think of rape as related in any way to sexual desire. The September 4, 1992, definition of rape as a crime of discrimination has been swept aside by the revelation of the Serb policy of genocidal rape and rape/death camps so that, in February 1993 Mazowiecki could write, in his report, "The Situation of Human Rights in the Territory of the Former Yugoslavia": "49. Rape is an abuse of power and control in which the rapist seeks to humiliate, shame, embarrass, degrade and terrify the victim. The primary objective is to exercise power and control over another person" (73).

This is a great accomplishment. It clarifies that a victim of rape need not be identified as belonging to a particular gender or to a particular sex. Anyone may be liable to be raped, as the Serb Brana Plan specifies ("women and children"—i.e., girls and boys—and, as it has turned out, also adult males). Thus "women," though we in fact constitute the overwhelming majority of rape victims globally, do not appear as the *natural* victims of this crime of violence. This definition also removes rape from any realm of sex (biological naturalness) or sexuality (the powerful workings of desire, used in some cultures to defend rapists and to demonize victims). It thus diminishes the possibility that rape of female persons by male persons might be considered natural, something desired by the victim, something that happens when the perpetrator is swept off his feet. By clearly stating that rape is an abuse of power and control, this definition forthrightly shows it to be a serious crime of violence.

Look at what remains, however. If rape is an "*abuse* of power and control," then some "power and control"—here based implicitly on gender—is itself implicitly legitimate. The good intentions behind Mazowiecki's enlightened definition of rape, even those evident at its conclusion, where the objective of the crime is defined in terms of power removed from any notion of appropriate and inappropriate exercise of power, are undermined by its use of the phrase "abuse of power and control." By itself, the term "abuse" implies what the definition's last sentence scrupulously avoids: the power and control evident in rape is an abusive version of power and control that in other circumstances are normal. Here again, therefore, the powerful effects of male gender supremacy make an appearance. It seems utterly impossible for even the most well intentioned international definitions of rape to avoid naturalized notions of male supremacy. The very mention of the word "rape" seems to set off the cliché: the image of male over female, in all senses of the word, still looks natural.

I have not found a totally satisfactory definition of rape, therefore, much less of genocidal rape, in any of the documents of international law I have studied, and certainly not in any of the conventions and protocols that serve as the basis of the proceedings of the United Nations tribunal in The Hague. Whichever Serbs, Bosnian Serbs, Croats, or Bosnian-Herzegovinian Catholic, Orthodox, or Muslim soldiers or militiamen are prosecuted for rape by the tribunal, they will be prosecuted as if they had all committed the same crime, an offense to "women's dignity," a crime of "discrimination" against "women."

Given this reality, how can I hope to find an adequate definition of the exacerbated form of rape that hundreds of thousands of persons have suffered because of the most bloodcurdling official policy since the Shoah?

I return to my analysis of genocidal rape. It is aimed primarily at Bosnian-Herzegovinian and Croatian women and children. This means that such women and children are raped in public in villages and towns. This means that Bosnian-Herzegovinian and Croatian women, children, and men are raped sporadically in concentration camps, as we have heard from countless testimonies. This means that Bosnian-Herzegovinian and Croatian women and girls are raped systematically in rape/death camps, sometimes within the confines of concentration camps, often elsewhere. This means that Bosnian-Herzegovinian and Croatian women and girls are systematically raped and then killed. This means that Bosnian-Herzegovinian and Croatian women and girls are forcibly impregnated, continually raped, and then expelled from the rape/death camps when their pregnancies have progressed beyond a point at which an abortion would be safe.

Wait a minute. Some women and girls in the rape/death camps are raped and then killed, whereas some are raped and impregnated. These women and girls generally are not killed. There is a difference between the kind of genocidal rape that ends in murder and the kind that ends in pregnancy: victims of the second kind of genocidal rape must be able to become, and remain, pregnant. Being a female, therefore, is a *necessary* condition for receiving this kind of treatment. *But it is not a sufficient one.* The second kind of genocidal rape in the rape/death camps, the kind aimed at enforced reproduction, demands that its victims be *persons capable of gestating a pregnancy.*

There are many women (to use the cultural, gender definition) and many females (to use the sexual one) who do not qualify, so to speak, for this particular, and particularly Serb, atrocity because, for any of a number of reasons, they do not get pregnant. They may be too young or too old. They may not ovulate. They may miscarry immediately. The human categories "woman" and "female" are full of persons whose biological capacities are other than that required for gestating a pregnancy.

So now I have pinned down the enforced-pregnancy version of this historically new crime to what I can only call its biological specificity: this version of genocidal rape is operable only on persons whose reproductive systems are capable of gestating a pregnancy. For such a person, being female is a necessary but not a sufficient identity. All definitions of rape that depend on normative or derivative versions of gender and sex, therefore, are inadequate as definitions of this form of genocidal rape. Whether they figured this out from the start or not, the Serbs who devised this atrocity have hoodwinked international war crimes conventions as they have hoodwinked international human rights legislation.

The Body and the Law

Or maybe not. Against all my feminist notions of what is right thinking about gender, against all my convictions that culture determines behavior quite entirely, I begin to wonder previously unthinkable things. If gender in international jurisprudence works as a reductive category ("women" being implicitly second-class humans and "natural" rape victims), and if the biological specificity I have isolated in genocidal rape for enforced pregnancy is a universal requirement for the implementation of that specific version of genocidal rape, can I find an adequate—even if not intentionally so—description of such genocidal rape elsewhere in international war crimes conventions and protocols?

Current protocols against war crimes and current human rights instruments leave a sieve of escape routes for whomever wishes not to face all the implications of the vicious, sexist specificity of genocidal rape. For the reasons I have mentioned, it is possible even to prosecute rapists as war criminals and never fully escape the masculinist mentality that in fact permitted such crimes in the first place. There are any number of ways such documents allow one to persist in thinking, clucking one's tongue all the while, that these are horrible crimes, the perpetrators are evil, the tribunal is doing well to prosecute them, *and* (1) it was ever thus, (2) the women asked for it, (3) *it happens to women over there and not to me,* and (4) *it is done by men over there and not by me.*

The holes in current international definitions, therefore, not only allow for the persistence of naturalized and gendered notions of rape, but they also encourage the notion of the specificity of the victim as well as the perpetrator as other, as if only Serb war criminals committed rape, as if only Bosnian-Herzegovinian Muslim women were victimized by it.

If, however, the specificity of the victim of genocidal rape aimed at enforced pregnancy derives precisely from one biological system, then any human being is virtually *like* that victim, because any human being has specific biological systems. Moreover, if I can find a definition of genocidal rape that concentrates on this universalizing particularity, I can short circuit centuries of patriarchal conditioning that makes rape a less-than-serious crime of sex relations where one gender or sex is often considered naturally dominant anyway. I can, in fact, begin to show how serious genocidal rape is, and how universal a menace it might be, by determining, as I encourage the judges of the United Nations International Criminal Tribunal to do, that it is a crime of *biological warfare.*

Biological Warfare

The definitions of biological warfare I have found are remarkably wary; each seeks to codify the myriad forms of such aggression now in use, but none is willing to be strictly limited. The resultant vagueness is an indication, I believe, of a menacing side of our contemporary dependence on, if not belief in, advanced scientific technology. Biological warfare seems, according to the definitions I have read, to be a burgeoning field, a form of warfare that may show vast development in the years ahead.

In spite of the very contemporary associations any definition of biological warfare carries with it, we would do well to remember that such warfare is not, by any means, new. The smallpox virus was used, for example, by eighteenth-century Europeans in North America, who gave utensils infected with smallpox to Native Americans (Veuthey, *Guérilla et droit humanitaire*, 81).[7]

In general, recent and present-day versions of biological warfare depend on the use of bacteriological or viral or some other living agents. When directed against an enemy target, such agents are intended to induce both short-term and long-term harmful effects on the persons who receive them. These effects often include the malfunction of a particular biological system (respiratory, muscular, or circulatory, for example), resultant short-term illness, immediate death, long-term illness, or death after long-term illness. A belligerent force might find such warfare efficient if it wished to severely harm or kill human and animal populations, and plant life, without damaging property. Nonetheless, biological warfare presents some grave difficulties that must be overcome if it is to be used to the desired effect. These include containment prior to delivery; delivery to a specific target; protection against "blowback"—where the agents, if aerosol, would literally be blown back on the attacking forces by currents of air— and against other forms of infection of the attacking forces.

The pithiest definition of biological warfare I have found is this: "A biological war is a voluntary use of living organisms or their toxic products with the aim of killing or harming persons, useful animals, or plants" (ibid.; my translation). The three elements central to this definition seem to me to pertain in all definitions and instances of biological warfare: (1) policy on the part of the attacker ("voluntary use"); (2) intent to kill or harm; and (3) victims defined biologically (as humans or other living beings) and not civically (as soldiers or civilians).

Other definitions, in their varied attempts to delineate biological warfare without limiting it to only the means already known, smack at times of cinematic drama. According to David Robertson's *Dictionary of Modern Defence and Strategy*, for example, biological warfare

> involves taking a highly infectious virus which occurs naturally and developing it so that its lethality is enormously increased. This would make it possible to infect large populations or large territorial areas with very small samples. Thus a war would be fought by deliberately infecting the enemy's armies or civilian population with deadly diseases, some of which, in their scientifically enhanced form, could kill in minutes. The ideal biological agent is one with a very fast infection and death rate, but which also becomes inert very rapidly, allowing troops to occupy the no-longer defended areas.

Unfortunately, we have no guarantees that such visions of scientists working to enhance the deadliness of viral infective agents are merely science fiction. Note, in this definition at any rate, the emphasis on the agent's rapidity of infection and death rate as well as the rapidity of its return to an inert state.

A NATO document elaborates biological warfare much more fully (NATO *Handbook on the Medical Aspects of NBC* [Nuclear, Biological, and Chemical] *Defensive Operations*). Three characteristics it notes are of particular relevance here: biological warfare is the use of a pathogenic microorganism to induce disease and to spread infections (1-2); "the susceptibility of the target population is an important factor in the selection of biological agents" (2-2); and "the selection of agents is expected to be made on the basis of technical as well as biological criteria" (2-1).

Biological warfare, as described officially by the Italian armed forces, demands the following characteristics of a biological weapon:

- heightened virulence;
- increased infectivity;
- high toxicity;
- brief incubation period, or one suited to operational goals;
- heightened capacity for stable storage;
- increased stability in aerosol form;
- heightened resistance to atmospheric agents;
- resistance to discovery/identification;
- ease of production in quantities that are significant from a military point of view;
- ease of dissemination;
- controllability of the spread of disease on the part of the attacker;
- scarce or no susceptibility to pharmaceutical, immunological, and prophylactic defenses. (Stato Maggiore, 24-25)

A description supplied to me by the Italian Society for International Organizations, but one neither Sara Cavelli nor I have yet been able to document beyond the fact that its format resembles that of other NATO documents, contains elements of all these characteristics. In a section titled "Biological Warfare Defined," it states:

> Biological warfare is the intentional use of living agents and toxins, such as bacteria, viruses, and other microorganisms or pathogens, to produce death or disability in man and animals, or to injure or destroy plants and other vegetation. The term "biological" is used here rather than "bacteriological" because it includes not only the use of germs but insect pests as vectors, or carriers, and other destructive agents. Biological warfare is a weapon primarily directed against persons, but it may be used against animals and plants. It does no structural damage to buildings or other inanimate objects. An enemy would employ biological warfare against us [a targeted population] to:
>   (1) reduce the means of making war by incapacitating personnel;
>   (2) reduce the will to war by adversely affecting the morale of personnel;
>   (3) reduce the means of making war by attacking livestock and destroying crops and agricultural products.

In the following section, titled "Biological Warfare Agents," this document emphasizes the diverse effects that biological warfare may intend, in particular those that are persistent as opposed to nonpersistent, and those that are permanent as opposed to temporary:

> 1. *Classification.* Biological warfare agents may be classified as persistent and nonpersistent. The persistent agents will remain effective for a long period and can be very much more resistant to the elements than even the most persistent chemical agents. This has obvious consequences both in attack and in defense. Biological agents may also be classified according to the degree of contagion

engendered. The major groups, based on their effects, are as follows:

(1) those that produce temporary incapacity only, although it may be of several weeks' duration;

(2) those that result in a high percentage of deaths or permanent disability.

2. *Characteristics.* The most important property of these living agents is their ability to multiply in the body of the person infected. This means that exceedingly small doses can produce disease, but sometimes the effects are delayed for days or even weeks while the organisms multiply. However, some germs are very sensitive to destructive influences, and this is a governing factor in determining their suitability for employment as biological warfare agents. In general, they are more susceptible than are chemical agents to the effects of heat, light, storage, and explosive forces. They present problems, therefore, both in storage and in dissemination as a weapon.

In a section titled "Possible Means of Attack," the document reiterates some of the difficulties that accrue to most biological warfare:

Although man, animals, and plants are subject to many diseases, careful study shows that, for one or more reasons, remarkably few pathogens are likely to be selected for use in war. Most agents are unsuitable because of (*a*) low, irregular, or undependable infecting power when exposed to air, (*b*) the natural or artificial resistance, or immunity, of the population, or (*c*) undue persistence of the agent for so long a period as to make occupation of the area impossible even for the using force. Probably not more than twenty species of disease-producing agents need be given close attention.

The faulty logic of the official Serb policy (although not, of course, the actual results of the Serb practice) would suggest twenty-one such agents. It should be clear by now that definitions of biological warfare, despite their generic use at times of the term "man" for "human" or "person," come closer to describing the biological specificity of genocidal rape—*which is also its criminal specificity*—than do definitions of rape in international conventions and protocols or human rights documents. Although historic use of biological agents in warfare may create the impression that such agents must be produced externally to the healthy human body, these definitions do not exclude internally produced agents. I would suggest, therefore, that, in spite of a general tendency not to think of it as a weapon of destruction, the faulty logic of the Serb policy views sperm in genocidal rape precisely as an agent of biological warfare.

The NATO *Handbook on the Medical Aspects of NBC Defensive Operations* of 1973 reinforces this conclusion. In the second chapter of its "Biological" section, "Characteristics of Biological Agents," in the paragraph on selection, we read:

a. Theoretically a considerable number of disease-causing microorganisms and toxins could be employed for military use in a biological weapons system. It is extremely difficult to list biological agents likely to be encountered since such a list would be both incomplete and erroneous.

b. The selection of biological agents is expected to be made on the basis of technical as well as biological criteria. The technical problems are mainly related to mass-production and storage. The problems involved in production of viruses are more complex than for bacterial agents. The agents most likely to be used are those already existing in nature since, in spite of important progress in the field of microbial genetics which has facilitated the selection of genetically modified agents, the possibility of creating entirely "new" agents by such procedures still seems remote. (2-1)

Regarding infectivity, the document states, "Agents intended for large-scale coverage should preferably possess a high degree of infectivity, that is, the minimum infective dose should be small" (2-1).

As for lethality, it notes, "Biological agents are categorized arbitrarily as lethal or incapacitating" (2-2). When considering the incubation period, it says: "For tactical purposes microorganisms producing disease with an incubation period greatly exceeding 24 hours would in most circumstances be undesirable because of lack of control once the weapon had been released" (2-2).

Finally, in a section titled "Other Characteristics," the handbook addresses one of the key aspects of genocidal rape: the vulnerable social position of the victims and the vast increase in this vulnerability when they are imprisoned in rape/death camps: "The susceptibility of the target population is an important factor in the selection of biological agents" (2-2).

A structural analysis of the effective elements of the Serb policy's logic (though not the actual results, babies who inherit genes equally from mother and father) of genocidal rape shows, therefore, that such rape qualifies as biological warfare for several reasons. First, as a systematic policy, it is willfully destructive and aimed at harming and, in fact, annihilating a human population. Second, it attacks a highly susceptible sector of that population—women and children, and sometimes men, who are under the threat of death, whether imprisoned or not. Third, like more traditionally imagined agents of biological warfare, sperm, as used in genocidal rape for enforced pregnancy, attacks a specific biological system in its victims: the reproductive system of persons capable of gestating a pregnancy. Fourth, genocidal rape has both immediate and long-term effects. Immediately, it produces atrocious physical pain, mental suffering, and often death; on a long-term basis, the version aimed at enforced reproduction produces pregnancy, possible social ostracism, severe psychological trauma, and possible death by abortion, suicide, or childbirth. On a long-term basis, it also produces unplanned children for whom material, social, and cultural accommodation must somehow be made, thus taxing the target population for years, if not generations, to come.

Genocidal rape qualifies as a crime of biological warfare not only because of its effects on its victims. As biological warfare, the use of sperm in genocidal rape not only is effectively destructive; it also constitutes a highly perfected form of biological warfare for its chemical stability, ease of storage, and capacity to deliver to a specific target. These solutions to the difficulties that plague other instances of biological warfare derive from the fact that the male human body is often a highly efficient producer, storer, and deliverer of sperm.

I am stating the obvious here, but I am stating it in a context that is not so obvious. The biological specificity of genocidal rape, particularly the version dependent on enforced pregnancy, necessitates this sort of displaced analysis of the means employed, which themselves are highly biologically specific.

Finally, the biological mechanisms of the production and delivery of the biological agent, sperm, used in the war crime of genocidal rape aimed at enforced pregnancy and reproduction, are such that the attackers need never fear the phenomenon of blowback. By definition, they can never get pregnant themselves.

I was speaking about this with a Croatian friend when she startled me by remarking that it was not so clear to her that the attackers who perpetrate genocidal rape would be protected against blowback. Granted, she said, they themselves would not be impregnated. But what would happen to them years from now, when the generation of babies created by this mass rape were adults? Would there not be a tidal wave of revenge? It all depends, I replied, on how the societies in which these children are raised represent the situation that produced them. And, from the point of view of the children, everything depends on whether their home societies accept the Serb ideology and consider them Serbs, and thus enemies, or whether they treat them as the innocent results of a policy for which they cannot be held responsible.[8]

Theme 6

IMPLICATIONS

National Identity

The events I have been discussing hold profound implications for current and future possibilities of social organization, not only in the countries immediately at stake, but also in the rest of the world. Clearly implicit in these events, for example, is a reevaluation of communal identity as national, and of national identity as congruent with that of a state. From the beginning of the "ethnic cleansing" of the Yugoslav National Army, a notion of the Serb people as a nation deserving power within the institutions of Yugoslavia has been operant. Then, with the independence of Slovenia, Croatia, and Bosnia-Herzegovina, those who subscribed to this notion of Serb national identity openly took up a campaign for what they claimed was legitimate sovereignty over all the territories of what had been Yugoslavia. Simultaneously, the declarations of independence of the three breakaway states were made in the name of national identities congruent with state power operant in already well-defined, and limited, regions. Much remains to be studied about these various regional renegotiations of cultural identity lived as national identity and then as nation-state formations. It behooves me to note here, at least, that the establishment of three new, internationally recognized states, as well as the extreme genocidal nationalism of the Belgrade government and the Bosnian Serb forces, are signs that traditional notions of national identity are taking on new values, and in many cases these values are radically different from what they might have been, say, in eighteenth-century Europe. In the four cases involved here, they correspond variously and at times simultaneously to liberal ideologies supporting state independence from a confederacy; the right to property, life, and liberty; democratic ideologies related to human rights; capitalist ideologies promoting free trade and participation in a competitive, non-state-controlled market economy; fascist ideologies of strong state control; racist ideologies proclaiming relative "ethnic" cleanliness and filth; and, quite to the point for my concerns here, sexist ideologies that reduce one gender and one sex to a means of genocide.

The emergent valorizations of national identity discernible in these events also demonstrate the overwhelming power of fear as a motivation for action. All the identities just mentioned, plus religious identity, function at times as categories for the distribution of fear, where one identity fears annihilation by another. Such fear is clearly justified in the case of the persons who have suffered Serb aggression in Bosnia-Herzegovina and Croatia and Croatian aggression in Bosnia-Herzegovina. It is also the hinge on which the discursive production of national identity turns and may be turned by those in power. Analyses of these phenomena are of the utmost urgency if we are to grasp the power and new malleability of national identity construction throughout the world.[1]

Western Morality

It can never again be said that the Western powers will surely intervene to stop genocide anywhere in the world, and particularly in Europe, whence a good portion of Western morality traditionally derives. It can never again be thought that the reason for nonintervention in the Shoah was lack of knowledge. Never before has so much information about a genocide in progress been consistently available to, and consistently ignored by, official state institutions. Lack of intervention to stop the genocide is a clear sign of the crisis, if not the end, of the moral and ethical systems upon which Western democratic institutions have historically been based. Any of us who are concerned about increasing democracy must understand this and call to task not only the war criminals but also those persons who make up Western governments.

International Institutions

The renegotiations of national identity and its relation to state sovereignty, as well as the severe crisis, if not collapse, of Western morality as evidenced by the events I have been discussing, contribute to a third phenomenon that has vast implications for future social organization on a global scale: the impotence of international institutions when faced with these new manifestations of nation-statehood. The tensile strength, so to speak, of governance and ethical systems upon which member states have been based is clearly shifting because of the end of the Cold War and because of postcolonial demographic patterns, for example. Historic notions of the nation-state, therefore, have proved to be insufficient guideposts for international intervention in this aggression. Conventions of chivalric warfare and gentlemanly diplomatic strategy and behavior have been blatantly undermined again and again by Karadžić and Milošević, who value Serb extremism far above international respect for gentlemanly comportment. International negotiators, all of whom have been male, have thus had a very difficult time, since at least two of the players won't abide by their code.

The United Nations has been stymied time and time again by its own lack of authority. Composed as it is of the very nation-states that are being reevaluated globally by their own constituents according to many of the issues at stake in this war— multiculturalism, religious identity and its role in the state, and gender justice, for example—the United Nations has as yet been unable to muster support for a clear and consistent policy toward an aggression its own charter defines as threatening to international peace (chapter 1, article 1, paragraph 1) and for which its own charter provides international (United Nations) authority to intervene (chapter 1, article 1, paragraph 1; chapter 7, article 42).

NATO has been suffering the same sort of institutional weakening. NATO, the United Nations, and all other international institutions must immediately look to the current reformulations of the historical foundations upon which their member states are based in order to discern whatever justification for and legitimation of their own existence and authority may yet remain. When such justification and legitimation are not evident, international organizations must discern the new formulations as they appear, and revamp, or in fact entirely reform, themselves accordingly.

The Privatization of Foreign Policy

An immediate result of the challenge this genocide poses for

Western ethical systems, and of the challenge this aggression poses for international as well as national organizations and governments, is that no Western state can convincingly claim any longer to embody a firm commitment to the moral and ethical foundations of human rights. While governments continue their business of foreign policy, therefore, citizens may now perceive with a clarity perhaps not available previously that this business of foreign policy has first and foremost to do with power relations and not with human rights. Such relations are apparently calculated according to information not widely, or perhaps not even publicly, available, so that U.S. foreign policy with regard to Bosnia-Herzegovina, for example, might be highly dependent on a calculation of effects on relations with China, say, but such calculations would neither be evident to U.S. media consumers nor represented in official discourse. In any case, official foreign policy on the part of the major European nation-states and the United States may now be more intent on forming public opinion than on discerning and reflecting it. On the other hand, public opinion in the United States and the major European countries may in fact be precisely reflected in official government policy: a temporarily troubled conscience followed by a media-padded conviction that nothing can be done.

Genocide in Europe today is a severe challenge to all existing European and United States democratic and human rights discourse. Official responses, at both the nation-state and international levels, have not stopped the genocide in spite of full knowledge of it and full intervention capacities—capacities that have been used elsewhere, as demonstrated in the Gulf War.

As for relief operations, the international organizations that have been politically impotent have in fact proved themselves capable of life-saving intervention on a wide, if not always sufficient, scale. Without appropriate military support, however, such humanitarian intervention is liable to political and military manipulation.

A remarkable fact of the history of humanitarian intervention since the beginning of the armed aggression is that so much of it has been accomplished by nongovernmental organizations. From the Red Cross and Red Crescent to grassroots groups in Italy, help originating in all the countries whose governments have been vacillating has been energetically forthcoming. I doubt that any conclusions can be drawn on the basis of this perception, but I for one have begun to wonder if foreign policy itself in the West, like industry in Eastern Europe, is not undergoing a process of privatization. Such a move may be implied in the contrasting dynamics of governmental nonintervention and private intervention we can discern in this war.

Genocidal Rape and Genetic Warfare

In theme 5, "Remedies," I gave two reasons why the United Nations International Criminal Tribunal should consider genocidal rape aimed at enforced pregnancy to be a crime of biological warfare. First, such reconceptualization emphasizes the universalizing specificity of the crime: it attacks one biological system of the victim in order to destroy a population. Thus the victim is identified not in a culturally variable way as only "woman," nor in a biologically deterministic way as only "female." By identifying the individual victim instead as a person capable of gestating a pregnancy, the notion of genocidal rape as biological warfare implicitly universalizes the victim, so that any human with any biological specificity, which of course includes all of us, is potentially victimized—*if not by this particular version of biological warfare, then by any number of other versions.* Second, to see that genocidal rape constitutes biological warfare emphasizes the seriousness with which the crime of rape should be treated; as biological warfare in the instance of genocidal rape for enforced pregnancy, the violent crime of rape departs from traditional contexts that limit it to a thing that often, and therefore "naturally," happens to women or females.

Another reason for treating such rape as biological warfare is that to do so places an emphasis on the genocidal intent of the aggressor and on aspects of the aggressor's official policy that hold terrifyingly ominous implications *because they might be used as precedents for future warfare that would no longer be biological but genetic.* Take, for example, the logic in the official Serb policy of the Brana Plan. According to this logic, various populations— Bosnian-Herzegovinian Muslims, Croats, and Jews, and Croatian Croats, for example—must be displaced and/or destroyed. This is to be accomplished by, among other things, mass rape, other torture, massacre, and *reproduction.* The logic of the policy depends on the perpetrators' (or the policymakers') conviction that offspring from Serb-other couplings will be entirely Serb in spite of the fact that the Serb father will have no part in the child's upbringing and Serb culture will provide no context for that child's acculturation. The implications are that genocidal rape functions as a mode of *genetic engineering* whereby the "desirable" Serb genes seek and destroy the "undesirable" other genes and any resultant children will therefore "naturally" be Serb. Therefore, although the Serb policy of genocidal rape for enforced pregnancy and reproduction depends on an ignorance of genetics, its most formidable implications may lie precisely in the degree to which it might serve as a precedent for genetic warfare: genetic engineering for purposes of genocide.

An ominous article appears in the 1993 SIPRI (Stockholm International Peace Research Institute) Yearbook, *World Armaments and Disarmament*. Coauthored by Tamas Bartfai, head of the Department of Neurochemistry and Neurotoxicology at the University of Stockholm, S. J. Lundin, retired senior director of research of the Swedish National Defense Research Establishment and former head of SIPRI's chemical and biological warfare program, and Bo Rybeck, director-general of the United Nations Food and Agriculture Organization (FOA) and former surgeon general of the Swedish armed forces, "Benefits and Threats of Developments in Biotechnology and Genetic Engineering" offers a brief panorama of presently available genetic techniques that might be used to produce new methods of warfare and mass extermination. In all cases, implementation would depend precisely on the kind of reasoning that is evidenced by the current Serb policy of genocidal rape for enforced pregnancy and reproduction.

After noting the potential for genetic weapons development that might accrue to "increased knowledge about the human genome and genetic diversity" (293-94) and noting that "it appears that such weapon development including the application of genetic engineering techniques took place on a large scale in the former Soviet Union" (294), the article mentions the project to map the human genome as being potentially danger-ridden as well as potentially helpful. It devotes most time, however, to an overview of current biotechnologies. These include the following:

- heterologous gene expression, described as "a widely applied technique to produce proteins in another organism than the one in which they are produced naturally" (295);

- genetically engineered (or "transgenic") organisms: "organisms which carry foreign DNA genes owing to artificial introduction of these by man, or organisms whose genetic make-up has been altered by human activity" (296);
- protein engineering, "a technique whereby the genes that code for particular proteins are modified so as to give rise to more active or functionally altered 'protein products' " (297);
- human monoclonal antibodies, whereby, "by use of a 'combinatorial library approach,' it is now possible to select human monoclonal antibodies to deadly toxins without having to expose a human being to these agents to initiate a human immune response *in vivo*" (298).

Bartfai, Lundin, and Rybeck go on to mention, as regards heterologous gene expression and protein engineering of toxins, that "the introduction into a bacterium or virus of genetic material (coding for virulence factors) which causes expression of toxic substances not normally existing in the strain could be applied to obtain new types of biological weapons" (302).

Such engineering could greatly reduce the cost of the manufacture of microorganisms as well as the creation of "organisms that produce a variety of toxins in addition to those normally produced by that micro-organism" (ibid.). Genetics technologies could produce a large variety of possible toxins, moreover, thus creating some of the same difficulties as those I noted earlier with regard to current biological weapons, especially those related to protective measures: "In any case, the means of production for such weapons could make effective export monitoring and control of dual-purpose equipment particularly problematic; similar difficulties could apply to purchases of material for vaccine production" (ibid.).

In response to the question "Can 'genetic weapons' be developed?" the article notes that such an idea is not new but dates from at least the mid-1970s (303). In order to be effective, such weapons would depend on clear population-group differences in "blood group proteins and histocompatibility proteins." The article notes that "dramatically different sensitivities to certain infectious agents have also been documented" in different population groups (the article calls these "races") (303). The Human Genome Project may determine a certain degree of variable population susceptibility; "such estimates range between 0.1 and 1 per cent" at present "but are very arbitrary" (303-4). The report goes on to state that "discernible ethnic differences are not distributed according to geographical and political borders in a way that would allow a particularly high degree of precision in choosing potential targets. It might be necessary for a user of genetic weapons to take risks with regard to his own and friendly populations" (304).[2]

The authors of this article clearly have the war and genocide in Bosnia-Herzegovina and Croatia in mind (304, 305 n. 45). This is particularly the case when they state that "today attempts at 'ethnic cleansing' are being carried out with seeming efficiency and impunity by the use of conventional weaponry" (305). Because they have not analyzed the gender, sex, and biological specificity of genocidal rape for reproduction, however, they do not see how this "conventional weaponry" includes the quite unconventional use of sperm as a biological weapon of mass destruction *according to a logic of genetic engineering.*

They have grasped, however, the "particularly detestable" aspect of this atrocity, even though they consider it only virtual and not already in progress. Perhaps in ignorance of the Serb policy of genocidal rape, they write, for example, that "it would be particularly detestable if biological or other weapons were developed which *utilize genetic characteristics as the basis for the effect of the weapons*" (ibid.). This is precisely what the Serb policy of genocidal rape claims; this is, in fact, the bedrock of its warped logic.

The Bartfai, Lundin, and Rybeck article is gravely concerned that current international treaties and protocols be enforced, in particular the Biological Warfare Convention of 1972 (294):[3]

> International efforts should continue in order to reinforce the current understanding that the BWC covers not only existing but also any possible future genetic weapons. This could usefully be reiterated at the next BWC Review Conference in 1996. Today attempts at "ethnic cleansing" are being carried out with seeming efficiency and impunity by the use of conventional weaponry. However, it is vital to recall that an international Genocide Convention does in fact exist. If it were implemented effectively, it would prohibit not only atrocities caused by conventional weaponry but also those caused by any method, old or new, *the aim of which is genocide or damage based on particular genetic characteristics.* (305; emphasis mine)

By now it should be clear that genocidal rape for enforced pregnancy and reproduction, the efficacy of which is based on particular biological characteristics (the victim's being female; the victim's capacity to gestate a pregnancy), may easily serve as a pretext for genetic warfare—*and in fact, given its logic, it already does.*

This kind of thinking must not be shuffled into the corners of a decaying ethics to gather dust as a futuristic phantasm or some fearsome science fiction. The global scourge of AIDS may already exemplify another instance of biological warfare that has gone uninterpreted as such, resulting in the vast destruction of human life. In any case, the Swedish researchers are aware of the dangers of voluntary blindness and a lack of interpretive imagination. They close their somber article, in fact, with an exhortation to interpretation: "Today it seems valid and urgent to reimplement the Genocide Convention, interpret its coverage and perhaps add interpretations that would explicitly prohibit preparation for genocidal actions, including the development and use of genetic weapons of any type, whether conventional, chemical or biological weapons" (ibid.).

My own work is intended as just such an added interpretation. It is offered with the greatest possible seriousness and urgency. The aggression must stop immediately. All rape/death camps and all concentration camps must be closed immediately. All war victims must be aided immediately. Reconstruction must begin immediately. A permanent International War Crimes Tribunal must be established immediately. The present United Nations International Criminal Tribunal must prosecute the crime of genocidal rape in all its manifestations and, in particular, it must consider prosecuting genocidal rape aimed at enforced pregnancy and reproduction as a portentous crime of biological warfare. Finally, I call upon each of my readers to contribute to the groups listed in the Appendix. Their task, and ours, is to aid the survivors, judge the perpetrators, and do anything else that will guard against such atrocity in the future. Thus shall we move toward new formulations of community and justice and peace.

NOTES

Introduction

1. Out of deference to her wishes, I indicate this friend not by her name but by the unrelated initial M. She is concerned that the appearance of her name in my text might jeopardize her work with survivors.

2. My clear recollection of this significant detail, which stunned me at the time, is in contrast with M.'s memory of these documents, which she recalls as having no photographs attached.

3. Cherif Bassiouni has investigated all reports of such videotapes and has been unable to ascertain whether any actually exist (personal communication). Véronique Nahoum-Grappe agrees with me that, whether they exist in fact or simply as rumor, even the rumor of such tapes is a chilling aspect of this genocide.

Theme 1. Identity

1. Because I can find no satisfactory scientific definition of "ethnicity" (although it is often used as if it stood for a particular genetic pool), because I consider it a strictly cultural category, and because there is no genetic differentiation between the "ethnicities" of the aggressors and the aggressed in this war, I put "ethnic" in quotes.

2. An influential defense of Croatian nationalism that emphasizes recent political history may be found in Finkielkraut.

3. For an excellent history of some of the cultural constitutions of binary-color racism, see Wheeler.

4. My brief historical sketch is drawn from numerous sources listed in Works Consulted. Foremost among these are Pirjevec, Riva and Ventura, and Weinberg and Wilsnack. I want to emphasize that there is nothing arcane or recherché about these sources; almost all are readily available in bookstores in Florence, for example. This is to say that anyone who cares to understand the available history of the Balkan peoples, which, like any other, will convey the perspectives of those who write it, may easily do so with market sources as well as with those available in libraries.

5. Most English-language commentators use the phrase, "Greater Serbia." Adnan Kemura, one of the leaders of the Bosnian-Herzegovinian community in Rome, admonishes me, however, to use the more literal "Great Serbia," as in "Great Britain," and I am happy to concede.

6. Philip Cohen, volunteer associate to the Bosnian-Herzegovinian Mission to the United Nations, explains: "As was true in Serbia, the Croatian puppet government was installed in power in 1941 by the Axis occupiers. . . . After Vladko Maček, the most popular leader in Croatia, had refused overtures from the Nazis to collaborate, . . . Hitler accepted Mussolini's suggestion to install his protégé Ante Pavelić to head the collaborationist Croatian government. . . . Pavelić had left Yugoslavia in 1929, the year Serbian King Aleksandar abolished all political parties, dissolved the assembly, and imposed a personal dictatorship. . . . The following year, Pavelić founded the extremist, nationalistic Ustasha movement, by organizing several hundred Croatian exiles in Fascist Italy, under the patronage and control of Mussolini. . . . The goal of the Ustashas was to achieve Croatian independence from Serbian rule, by any necessary means, including terror. . . . In 1934, King Aleksandar was assassinated by a Macedonian, in a conspiracy linked to Italy and the Ustashas. . . .

"Ustasha, therefore, was an extremist, ultranationalist organization committed to the realization of a Croatian state independent of Serbian rule, by any means, including the use of terror. Ustasha existed in exile in fascist Italy for more than a decade under the sponsorship and control of Mussolini, until their leader Ante Pavelić was installed to power by Hitler at Mussolini's suggestion. Most important, however, and generally overlooked, Ustasha does not have its roots in Croatia proper, nor did Ustasha obtain significant support from Croatia proper. Ustasha was rooted in western Herzegovina, an isolated, mountainous region generally populated by poorly educated, impoverished ethnic Croats. Sixty percent of Ustasha and most of the leadership came from here.

"Even until 1941, Ustasha did not incorporate ideological anti-Semitism (see the *Encyclopedia of the Holocaust*). Ustasha simply wanted independence so passionately that no price was too great. If their benefactors (the Nazis) wanted the Jews as the price of doing business, the Ustashas (as you see, I use this anglicized plural form) were ready to deliver them.

"It is noteworthy that Mate Boban and his followers from western Herzegovina display much of the same primitivism and provincialism as their brethren of fifty years ago. Regrettably, in 1993, these western Herzegovinian Croats, who exert so much influence on the Zagreb government (it is largely Herzegovinians in diaspora that financially support [Croatian president Franjo] Tudjman), are once again bringing enormous dishonor to Croatia. Finally, I must say this: I have many contacts among the intellectual community of Croatia, and they are appalled at the current direction of the government. I believe that most Croats in Croatia do not share the outlook of the Herzegovinians" (personal communication, August 3, 1993; see also Philip Cohen, *Desecrating the Holocaust: Serbia's Exploitation of the Holocaust as Propaganda* [typescript, 1994]).

7. Cohen elaborates: "Once installed into power, Pavelić's deplorable Ustasha regime undertook the extermination of Jews, based upon the German model, under German supervision. . . . In Ustasha concentration camps, Jews, Serbs, Gypsies, and anti-Ustasha Croats were savagely tortured and murdered. . . . Out of the 40,000 Jews in the Independent State of Croatia, 30,000 perished, 20,000 at the Jasenovac concentration camp. . . . Some perished on the Isle of Pag, . . . and as many as 9,500 were deported to Auschwitz. . . .

"Despite the complexity of events within Axis-occupied Yugoslavia, Serbian popular belief substituted a greatly simplified portrait, which emphasized the collective guilt of Croats for genocide in the Second World War, contrasted with the collective innocence of Serbs. . . . The Nazi collaboration of the Serbian government, many Serbian Orthodox clergy, and the Chetniks was conveniently ignored. At the same time, the Ustasha legacy was generalized to the whole of the Croatian people, . . . even though no more than a few percent of the Croat population participated in the Ustasha movement, . . . even though Croats led and supported the resistance, and even though the overwhelming majority of Croats were appalled at the activities of the Ustashas. . . .

"The deceptive logic of [present-day] Serbian propagandists can be summarized: Croatia was 'independent' and therefore Croats were collectively responsible for the Holocaust, . . . while Serbia was 'occupied' and therefore Serbs were collectively absolved of responsibility for the fate of Serbia's Jews. To strengthen their case, Serbs even argue that their primary role was to protect the Jews from harm. Indeed, Jews were variously sheltered and saved by Serbs, Croats, Muslims, and others. There are, however, significant omissions to the Serbian 'epic recitation' of the Second World War. Under the pro-Nazi government of Milan Nedić, Serbs collaborated with the Nazis in disseminating anti-Jewish propaganda, in plundering Jewish property, in delivering Jews for execution, and in murdering Jews in concentration camps. Dimitrije Ljotić had advocated the extermination of Jews for years before the Holocaust, and his collaboration with the Nazis, dating to early 1935, . . . was as voluntary as that of Ante Pavelić. Chetnik leader Draža Mihailović exercised his own free will when he ordered the extermination of all Muslims in the envisaged Greater Serbia. Many Chetniks knowingly delivered Jews to their death for a cash bounty. Indeed, the Ustashas and Chetniks were moral equivalents in their brutality, bloodlust, and criminality. Meanwhile, the most striking aspect of the resistance in occupied Serbia, from late 1941 until mid-1944, was its paucity" (ibid.).

8. "Chetnik" is the term Serbs use to designate irregular ultranationalist Serbian soldiers and, by extension, Serbian soldiers in general. This designation precedes World War I, deriving from a period when it was used for guerrilla bands organized primarily against Turks and, by association, any Muslim. Monarchists in the Serb military during World War II adopted the appelation "Chetnik," and initially resisted the Nazi occupation with the help of secret aid from Britain. When the Allies supported Tito's Partisans, who were fighting for a unified Yugoslavia, the Chetnik troops joined with those of the Nazi occupation. Genocidal Chetnik actions during World War II were directed against Muslims, Croats, Jews, Romani, and Communist Partisans. A traditional "trademark" of Chetniks, who are by definition male, is a long beard (Magas, 26, 296, 314-15, 317, 324; Weinberg and Wilsnack, 2).

9. This has been noted by other scholars as well. Regarding Ante Pavelić's ultranationalist, fascist Ustasha organization, for example, Cohen writes: "Most of Pavelić's followers drew from a similar background: 95% of the Ustasha exiles were peasants, workers, or sailors, mainly from the Dinaric Mountains of western Herzegovina" (personal communication, August 3, 1993).

10. Neither in Italy nor during any of my trips to Croatia have I been able

to locate a copy of Karadžić's "burn" poem. Many of the Bosnian-Herze-govinians with whom I have spoken are well acquainted with it, however. So, it would seem, is a poetry prize jury in Moscow; in the summer of 1994, Karadžić received the Russian Sholokhov Prize for his poetic achievements. Another Serb whose literary production has proved prophetic is Vuk Draš-ković, charismatic head of the ultranationalist opposition (to the ultra-nationalist government) in Belgrade. Drašković is the author of a novel de-picting the ritualized method of slaughtering civilians by slitting their throats. This novel, the French translation of which leaves out the more damningly ex-plicit gore (Véronique Nahoum-Grappe, 66), is entitled *The Knife*. An unex-purgated French translation is due to be published soon (ibid.).

11. In spite of such oversights, all too common in any patriarchy, the Granić et al. "book of evidence," which is based on evidence collected by the Division of Information in the Croatian Ministry of Health, provides what may well have been the most extensive published documentation of war crimes available at the time it was published in 1992.

12. I met Ms. De Filippis in the spring of 1992, when I went to Pescara to speak about these matters at the invitation of the Margaret Fuller feminist group. Dr. Maristella Lippolis, one of the leaders of the group and the presi-dent of the Abbruzzi Region Equal Opportunity Commission, came to Zagreb for the "Women, Culture, War" conference. Feminist women from Pescara have been engaged in fund-raising for survivor aid groups and other survivor support activities since then. The Margaret Fuller group in Pescara is a good example of how the war has concretized much feminist theory by necessitating a shift to theoretically motivated practice.

Theme 2. Representation

1. For examples of other decisions regarding the issue of the representa-tion of these atrocities, see the essays in Alexandra Stiglmayer's book, several of which narrate particular atrocities, sometimes in highly dramatic fashion. In her own article in the book she has edited, Véronique Nahoum-Grappe has decided not even to list the atrocities, as any such representation (1) is in and of itself a cruel gesture toward those who receive it, (2) is not neutral but instead always evokes powerful feelings that can be manipulated, and there-fore (3) resembles all propaganda, and in particular that of Serb president Slobodan Milošević since 1986 (Nahoum-Grappe, 46).

2. Personal communication, Zagreb, November 16, 1993.

3. According to Professor Marguerite Waller of the University of California at Riverside, a Budapest newspaper reported in 1993 that police in southern California had confiscated some of these tapes. I have been unable to confirm this.

4. A few weeks later (May 1994), a conference organized by the Italian Institute of Culture in Zagreb and the Istituto Gramsci in Venice, of Italian, Bosnian-Herzegovinian, and Croatian artists, philosophers, and writers, and held in Venice, Italy, met to discuss creativity in borderline situations and in states of emergency. The Italians' overwhelming lack of information about the aggression and the genocide made for a particularly embarrassing atmosphere. On top of that, some of the Italian participants began to refer to the papers delivered by the Bosnian-Herzegovinian and Croatian participants as "testimonies," whereas what they were offering was actually analysis and theory. This went so far as one of them offering a compliment to me, the sole U.S. conferee (and one of only two female participants, the other of whom had been asked to serve mostly as a translator), for the eloquence of *my* "testimony"—I, who had never seen or experienced anything to *testify* about. It seems that as soon as one begins to discuss the atrocities, no matter how careful, analytic, and theoretical one is, one's discourse is swept into the vast, tragic, and brimful category of "testimony," where it supposedly increases the mass of evidence but simultaneously renders its own force vestigial. I should also add that the thoughtful analysis offered at this conference by Nenad Popović of the political, philosophical, military, and semantic ironies of the aggression in general was also called an "eloquent testimony" by some of the Italians. By the end of the weekend, these same Italians had begun to realize the vast consequences of their own lack of information. One Venetian painter in particular, who had presented an intricate Heideggerian reading of violence and modesty in the slashed canvases of the Italian painter Fontana, became hesitant in his insistence that a slashed canvas was the most violent gesture possible when he learned that slashed throats are the most common mode of Chetnik and Serb slaughter.

5. Branca Rocchi, personal communication, Zagreb, November 14, 1993.

Theme 3. Facts

1. Popović directs Éditions Durieux, a prolific literary publishing house in Zagreb.

2. In addition to noting the systematic nature of (genocidal) rape perpe-

trated by various Serb forces (and civilians), the Bassiouni Report, in section E, "Detention Facilities," while failing to remark the specific characteristics of the Serb-run rape/death camps, nonetheless does note the following:

"218. Of the 715 camps: 237 were operated by Bosnian Serbs and the former Republic of Yugoslavia; 89 were operated by the Government and army of Bosnia and Herzegovina; 77 were operated by Bosnian Croats, the Government of Croatia, the Croatian Army and the Croatian Defence Council; 4 were operated jointly by the Bosnian Government and Bosnian Croats; and 308 camps for which it is not known with certainty under whose effective control they were.

"224. As the following discussion indicates, the number of camps and the number of reported violations in camps controlled by the Government of Bosnia and Herzegovina and its army are by far the lesser of the warring factions, irrespective of the ethnic or religious background of the detainees they hold. The number of reported violations by the Croatian Government, the Croatian Army and the Croatian Defence Council is larger, particularly against Serbs in Krajina and in eastern and western Slavonia and against Muslims from Bosnia and Herzegovina in Herzegovina. . . .

"227. Bosnian Government camps are reported to have been the site of cases of grave breaches of the Geneva Conventions. These allegations include killing and torture of Croatian and Serbian prisoners. The number of reports and allegations are, however, limited. The Commission has not been able to detect any particular pattern or policy of wrongdoing. The Commission has, however, ascertained that the Goverment of Bosnia and Herzegovina has expressed its opposition to these individual violations.

"228. The Bosnian-Croat and Croatian Defence Council camps were in Herzegovina. The Croatian Government and Croatian Army operated camps were in the Krajina area, in eastern and western Slavonia and in other parts of Croatia. Grave breaches of the Geneva Conventions have occurred in these facilities against Serbs and Bosnian Muslims, including killing, torture and rape. The Commission has not been able to detect any particular pattern or policy in operating these camps. The Commission has information concerning the location and some information about the physical layout and command structure of some of these camps. The Commission also has information concerning the killings and torture inflicted on the interned population, as well as the names of some perpetrators and victims. The largest number of violations reported are in the Krajina and eastern and western Slavonia against Serbs and in Herzegovina by Bosnian Croats and the Croatian Defence Council against Bosnian Muslims. The Government of Croatia has, since late 1993, according to information received by the Commission, condemned these violations and sought to curb their occurrences.

"229. The Commission has information that Bosnian Serbs are operating camps where grave breaches of the Geneva Conventions and other violations of international humanitarian law, including killing, torture and rape reportedly occur on a large scale. These camps are mostly in Bosnia and Herzegovina and hold Bosnian Muslims for the most part, but also Bosnian Croats. The Bosnian Serbs use camps to facilitate territorial and political control of a geographic region and to expel and eliminate other ethnic and religious populations from that area. The Commission has detailed information concerning some of the locations and physical layouts of some of these camps, including descriptions of the various buildings where prisoners are detained, interrogated, tortured and killed. The Commission also has information about some camp commanders and military units in the areas and individual violators."

This section of the report, entitled " 'Bosnian Serb Republic' camps," goes on for two pages to describe the criminal treatment of prisoners by Serb captors, treatment that often includes rape. Rape is so prevalent a crime in the camps, in fact, that the report devotes the entire following section to "Rape and other forms of sexual assault." The final paragraph of the section devoted to " 'Bosnian Serb Republic' camps," however, stands in marked contrast to the report's conclusions about the Croat- and Bosnian-run camps:

"231. The Commission concludes that grave breaches of the Geneva Conventions and other violations of international humanitarian law have been committed over a long period of time, on a large scale, and very frequently in the most brutal, inhuman and degrading manner. These violations are ordered by or known to the camp commanders, the local political leadership and police. Army units may or may not be involved. However, they do not intervene to stop these violations, thereby implying responsibility by omission."

3. Information documenting Serb-run concentration camps in Bosnia-Herzegovina was available to the United Nations Security Council at least by July 31, 1992, in a letter dated July 29 from Muhamed Sacirbey, ambassador and permanent representative of Bosnia-Herzegovina to the United Nations. In that letter, Sacirbey presented the Security Council with a list of the concentration camps and prisons in Bosnia and Herzegovina, Serbia and Montenegro, that were under the control of the Belgrade regime and its surro-

gates. He made an urgent appeal for action by the Security Council in order to "secure the safety of and make available basic needs" to the "innocent victims, so they can eventually return to their homes, as agreed in the London Agreement of 17 July." The text of this letter, along with translated Croatian media reports of the Serb-run camps practicing genocidal rape, was available in a media packet prepared by the Northern California Office of Croatian Affairs during the summer of 1992.

4. For an Italian translation of this "memorandum," see Accademia Serba delle Scienze e delle Arti (233-45).

5. "Nationalism was made from the top; its main authors were politicians. The main reason for the current crisis, which has many dimensions, is found in the defeat nationalism has inflicted on socialism," (ibid. 242). "The current condition, scarcely favorable to the Serb people, as are the increasingly violent demonstrations of chauvinism and Serbophobia, leads to a renewal and ever more evident manifestation of the national resentment of the Serb people and to reactions that can ignite the powder keg and that are thus dangerous. It is our duty not to ignore or underestimate these dangers. But at the same time we cannot accept the ideological and political assignment of historic fault being played out in the fight of principle against Serb nationalism" (243; my translation).

6. In a chapter entitled simply "Chetnik," Zaccaria recounts a White Eagles initiation ceremony that he infiltrated. Initiates swear their allegiance, under an uplifted sword, to "fight with all [their] strength for the Holy Sava, the pure Orthodox church, and the Unified Serbian State" (47). The Bassiouni Report describes this and other "special forces" in two significant paragraphs:

"121. There are 45 reported special forces, which usually operate under the command of a named individual and apparently with substantial autonomy, except when they are integrated into the regular army's plan of action. The special forces are supplied and often trained by the respective Governments that they serve. Many special forces answer only to senior political officials in the respective Governments. Such a relationship is frequently based on political allegiance and is not always publicly known. However, in time, information about the political sponsorship and support of these groups will become available. As these units usually operate independently and outside the apparent chain of command, their order of battle is not known. Notwithstanding the strong links between these units and the respective armies, the regular army failed to restrain them from the commission of grave breaches of the Geneva Conventions and other violations of international humanitarian law. Among the most notorious of the special forces are Arkan's 'Tigers' and Šešelj's 'White Eagles' (also referred to as 'Chetniks'). Lastly, many of these units operate throughout the territory of the former Yugoslavia. Thus, the Serbian units operate in Bosnia and Herzegovina and Croatia, and the Croatian units in Bosnia and Herzegovina. These special forces have committed some of the worst violations of international humanitarian law."

"139. Special forces . . . frequently carry out 'ethnic cleansing.' These forces clearly seem to be supported, equipped and supplied by the Governments they serve and are allowed to operate without control by the authorities in charge. Two particular groups of special forces that have committed the largest number of reported violations are Arkan's Tigers and Šešelj's White Eagles."

I would simply note that both groups singled out here are composed of Bosnian Serbs. The endnotes of the Bassiouni Report include further relevant information:

"24. Some of these special forces operate in localized areas, while others move freely to different theatres of operation, frequently going from one state to another within the territory of the former Yugoslavia. Several of the special forces come from Serbia proper or have close links to Serbia, like Arkan's 'Tigers,' Šešelj's 'White Eagles,' Captain Dragan's forces, Serb Falcons (Siniša Vučinić) and others. The Serbian People's Renewal Party also had a paramilitary organization which interrelated with the White Eagles. Serbian special forces from Krajina, like 'Martić's Militia,' operate predominantly in the UNPAS [United Nations Protected Areas] (Croatia). Other special forces from Croatia are tied to the Croatian government's political and army figures. The HOS [Croatian Defense Union], which is reminiscent of the Second-World-War Ustachi, for example, have been substantially absorbed into the Croatian Defence Council. The mujahidin operate independently of the Bosnian Government Army. Muslims from Bosnia and Herzegovina formed paramilitary units in 1991. Two such Muslim groups are called Green Berets and the Patriotic League of the People. All special forces have expatriate volunteers and some use foreign mercenaries.

"25. Arkan's name is Zeljko Raznjatović. Interpol has several outstanding warrants for his arrest. The warrants are for a variety of crimes, including bank robbery and investigations relating to political assassination in different European countries. He escaped from prison on bank robbery charges in the Netherlands and Sweden, where he is currently a wanted criminal. He is reputed to have been involved in murder for hire and to have connections with organized crime in Europe. His group has committed the entire range of crimes described above and in other parts of this report in Croatia and Bosnia and Herzegovina. The Tigers have used expatriates and mercenaries in the commission of these crimes. JNA [Yugoslav National Army] seems to arm and support the Tigers. The crimes committed by this group started in 1991 in the war in Croatia. In 1992, Arkan was elected to the Kosovo 'parliament' and ran in the 1994 parliamentary election of the Federal Republic of Yugoslavia in Belgrade. He has reportedly acquired substantial wealth in Sector East UNPA Croatia and in Belgrade which it is believed he derived from looting and contraband.

"26. Šešelj was a member of the parliament of the Federal Republic of Yugoslavia and leader of the ultra-nationalist Serbian Radical Party, which at one time held one third of the votes. Šešelj's group follows the pre-Second-World-War group called the 'Chetniks' who were known for their ultra-right wing monarchial politics. The Second-World-War Chetniks wore the special monarchial emblems with the double-headed eagle. The present forces wear the same emblem and also call themselves Chetniks. Like Arkan's Tigers, Šešelj's White Eagles committed the crimes referred to above and in other parts of this report. The group seems to have been armed and supported by JNA. Moreover, since mid-1993, the group is believed to have been under the direct control of JNA. The crimes committed by this group started in 1991 in the war in Croatia. During the 1993 elections in Belgrade, Šešelj and President Slobodan Milošević publicly traded charges of war crimes and hinted at knowledge of war crimes. This was publicly reported in the media of the Federal Republic of Yugoslavia in October 1993. It was also reported that President Milošević ordered some forty associates of Šešelj to be prosecuted for rape and other war crimes. It should also be noted that there were several groups of Chetniks that were not under Šešelj's control. One such unit operated in the Krajina area in Croatia in 1991, and then in Bosnia in 1992, where the group took position around Sarajevo in the fall. The unit is under the command of Slavko Aleksić, who operated under the command of the Bosnian Serb Army."

7. The Bassiouni Report categorizes the rapes somewhat differently, dividing them into five patterns. The first is rape performed by individuals or small groups before any fighting occurs; the second is public rape related to fighting; the third is rape by individuals or groups within "detention" camps; the fourth is rape as "ethnic cleansing," including rape that results in

pregnancy; the fifth is rape performed in forced brothels (what I and others call rape/death camps) for the purpose of entertaining soldiers. This pentapartite categorization, while it does note specific situations in which rape occurs, fails to adequately articulate the genocidal nature of *all forms* of rape as practiced even according to the five categories employed here.

8. See, in particular, her testimony to the journalist Roy Gutman in February 1993 ("One by One: The Ordeal of Women Raped and Beaten in Bosnia Camp," *New York Newsday*, reprinted in Gutman, 144-49).

9. The Omarska camp is known to the rest of the world better than are any of the other camps because pictures of it appeared in Western European and U.S. media in February 1993. You may recall the footage of emaciated men sleeping on the floor of what looks like a barn, or emaciated men standing blank-eyed behind chain-link and barbed-wire fences. These images, which recall those of Nazi concentration camps, gave many viewers the impression that somehow these were prisoners of war who earlier as soldiers had participated in armed combat and thus were liable to be captured. Most, in fact, were civilians. In any case, the images imply quite clearly that all the prisoners at the Omarska concentration camp were male. As it turns out, such was not the case.

10. A partial list of rape/death camps in Bosnia-Herzegovina was published as an appendix to the 1993 book *Violentate*, discussed in theme 2, "Representations." I reproduce that list here:

In central Bosnia and the Sarajevo region: Vraca, Ilijaš, Vogošča, Pale, Sokolac, and Han-Pijesak.
In eastern Bosnia: Foča, Čajniče, Višegrad, Zvornik, Bratunac and Bijeljina, Lomnica near Šekovići.
In northern Bosnia: Brčko, Brezovo Polje, Bosanski Šamac, Doboj, Teslić, Šipovo, the Majevica and Ozren mountains.
In the Bosnian Krajina: Lušci Palanka, Prijedor, Sanski Most, Jasenica near Bosanska Krupa, Bosanski Petrovac, Ripać near Bihać, the Grmeč and Kozara mountains.
In eastern Herzegovina: Nevesinje, Bileća, Trebinje. (117-18)

At a conference in Frankfurt in October 1994, I learned from Dr. Kozarić-Kovačić that pregnant survivors recently released from rape/death camps continue to arrive in Zagreb. This not only indicates that rape/death camps, about which nothing or next to nothing has appeared in the international media for months now, still exist; it also indicates that they have been, in fact, normalized.

11. The Agora Information Service is a transnational news information service run by the Transnational Radical Party based in Rome. The Transnational Radical Party ("radical" in the sense of rooted in specific issues, according to its secretary, Emma Bonino, at a news conference at the United Nations in April 1993) has been the single most effective transnational lobby at the United Nations for the establishment of the International Criminal Tribunal. It now supports the transnational "No Peace Without Justice" Committee's campaign to establish a permanent war crimes tribunal.

12. Further indication of the prevalence of genocidal rape by means of enforced pregnancy is found in abortion statistics. Mazowiecki reports as follows:

Croatia: "15. According to data obtained in one of the two major hospitals visited in Zagreb, 6,521 infants were delivered and 4,615 abortions performed in 1992. In the second hospital, 4,039 infants were delivered and 4,100 abortions performed in 1992 (as compared to 3,103 deliveries and 3,000 abortions in 1991). In both hospitals, the total number of abortions and deliveries increased in 1992. However, the ratio of abortions to deliveries remained approximately the same as in 1991, according to the physicians in charge of both hospitals' gynecology departments."

Bosnia and Herzegovina: "16. In 1992, the number of abortions performed at the clinic visited by the team of experts in Sarajevo had doubled in September, October and November (400-500/month) compared to pre-war rates (approximately 200/month). At the same time, the number of patient visits decreased by half. This means that there were effectively four times the number of abortions in those months compared to pre-war rates. Doctors noted an increase in late terminations of pregnancy beginning in September 1992.

"17. Spontaneous abortions (miscarriages) also increased in Sarajevo. This was thought to be due both to lack of availability of food as well as to psychological trauma.

"18. Abortions were performed at three health centres and several emergency centres in Sarajevo. However, some of these centres have been destroyed, along with all of their medical records" (66).

Federal Republic of Yugoslavia [Serbia-Montenegro]: "21. Despite a decline in live births, numbers of early and late abortions remained relatively stable from 1984 to 1992 at one of two specialist maternity hospitals in Belgrade.

The ratio of abortions to deliveries ranged between 0.5 and 0.7 between 1984 and 1992. A total of 4,200 early, and 438 late abortions were performed at this hospital in 1992. During the same year, 238 applications for late abortions were received by the Appeals Commission for the entire city" (67).

13. Simple lack of trust in their interlocutors may also be a factor in survivors' hesitancy to relate their experiences. I discuss a possible instance of this later, in Theme 4, "Analysis."

14. Section F, including paragraphs 232-53.

15. In Italy, I have seen television interviews with survivors of this horrible crime. I have also heard female survivors speak of castrations they were forced to witness or perform. One moving testimony from a male survivor is found in the Lončarević videotape.

16. One such photograph is found in the Italian newspaper *La Repubblica* (August 6, 1994, p. 28), where it is mistakenly identified as "the Nazi salute." Television coverage of Russian troops joining Unprofor in Bosnia-Herzegovina in 1995 shows Russian soldiers giving the Serb salute from their armored cars as they pass cheering Bosnian Serb soldiers. To my knowledge, no U.S. media commentator was aware of the significance of this gesture.

17. Fortunately, Drašković's movement is not the only Serb opposition to the government of Milošević and its genocidal policies. Although many oppositional Serbs would remain in Serbia-Montenegro now only at grave risk to their lives, a number of them, from the relative safety of Paris, for example, are active in antigovernment and antinationalist-extremist movements.

18. In spite of repeated attempts to obtain a videocassette of this film, I have as yet been unable to view it. Véronique Nahoum-Grappe describes a scene of throat slitting as being highly ritualized, and the procedure resembles what survivors have often described as the method used in the camps (Nahoum-Grappe, 66 n. 24).

19. Zaccaria speaks about a videotaped interview made by Croatian soldiers of a Bosnian Serb concentration camp guard they had captured. In a surprising turn during the questioning, the Serb explains flatly that, while he raped more than a dozen women, the main task assigned to him by Arkan's "Tigers" and Šešelj's "White Eagles" at the camp was that of "throat-slitter." In the evenings he would be called upon to slit the throats of the prisoners—men and women of all ages, all of them civilians. He recounts his method, which is exactly the ritual one others have testified to on so many occasions. One variant, however, as he went about his business of slitting the

throats of a total of eighty or so civilians, was that he would use a mason's mallet to hammer in the point of the knife before he drew it across their throats. When asked if he regretted his actions and whether he still felt like a man, he answered yes to the first question and, to the second, no (Zaccaria, 73-82).

20. As the most American-style hotel in Zagreb, the Intercontinental is host to a wide array of guests, including international journalists, arms dealers, UN soldiers, Croatian military commanders, and visiting feminist intellectuals.

21. I was living in Bari that year and playing in the Bari Symphony Orchestra. One young middle-class woman I met knew how to obtain such surgery.

Theme 4. Analysis

1. This age-old analogy between women's bodies and territory, and its connection to imperialist practices of conquering and colonization, is glaringly evident in John Donne's early seventeenth-century love poem, "Elegie: Going to Bed": "Licence my roaving hands, and let them go, / Behind, before, above, between, below. / O my America! my new-found-land, / My kingdome, safeliest when with one man man'd, / My Myne of precious stones: My Emperie, / How blest am I in this discovering thee! / To enter in these bonds, is to be free; / Then where my hand is set, my seal shall be" (in John Shawcross's edition of *The Complete Poetry of John Donne* [Garden City, N.Y.: Doubleday, 1967], 58).

2. The Bosnian-Herzegovinian Muslim family in Turin mentioned in Theme 3, for example, gives the lie to the demonic Islamic patriarch image she implies.

3. For a review of other instances of mass wartime rape, see Seifert.

4. This is a common reaction, by the way, according to Dr. Kozarić-Kovačić of the Vrapče Hospital in Zagreb and Dr. Sarajlić of the Ruke [hands] relief organization. See also Folnegović-Smalc.

5. In contrast to her fame in Western Europe and the United States as the most significant—if not the only—Croatian feminist, she is thought of by some Croatian nationalist women in Zagreb as a rank opportunist. These women tell me that Drakulić never worked for women's issues before the war, even though she was in a privileged position to do so. They feel she deserted her culture when the war began to find fame and perhaps even for-

tune as a self-styled representative of "ex-Yugoslavia" women and a best-selling explicator of the war in her *Balkan Express*. Anticommunists themselves, these women find Drakulić's privileges under Tito highly suspect. She also has her defenders in Zagreb, some of whom consider themselves pacifists. Unfortunately, to argue for an unconditional end to the war may be to ignore genocidal consequences. It is important to remember that in this war words have peculiar meanings. To be a pacifist now may mean to accept borders determined by Serb aggression and thus to facilitate the mass murder, according to Serb military policy, of non-Serbs living in territory taken by the Serbs.

6. Véronique Nahoum-Grappe notes the role of alcohol in the rapes recounted by survivors (Nahoum-Grappe, 58 n. 16).

7. As I mentioned in theme 1, "Identity," "ustasha" is the name of the political party in power in Croatia during World War II that collaborated with the German Nazis and the Italian fascists. During the current war, the term is used by Serbs to describe women and men who are Muslim or Catholic in Bosnia-Herzegovina and Croatia (MacKinnon, "Turning Rape into Pornography"; Magas).

8. The Serb novelist and politician Vuk Drašković provides a glimpse of this sort of thinking in an interview entitled "Darko Nudelist: u sjeni noza. Rozgovor s vukom Drašković," which appeared in the Zagreb journal *Start* on September 16, 1989 (51-57). Speaking of "perspectives of or for Yugoslavia in 1989," Drašković said: "If Yugoslavia disintegrates, the western borders of Serbia will have to be redefined according to principles of natural and historic law and based on the ethnic map that has been valid since April 6, 1941 (the date of Hitler's attack on Yugoslavia). Why do we go back to this precise date and these borders? Because during the Second World War the Croatian and Muslim Ustashas in these regions committed genocide against the Serbian people. If Yugoslavia disintegrates and there is a referendum, it will be up to the victims from Jasenovac, Jadovno, and Glina, from all Herzegovina's caves, from the Like and the region of Kordun to decide where to draw the western borders of Serbia. And not only up to them, but up to all their unborn descendants, too, who have also been vanished in those concentration camps. Or Ante Pavelić already defined those western Serbian borders, because Serbia exists where the largest Serbian concentration camps were, the biggest Serbian execution fields, the burned-out Serbian churches and villages. Wherever blood was flowing from Ustasha knives, precisely there is the western border of Serbia" (translated by Nenad Popović and Wolfgang

Klotz). There is a curious slip in this quotation: Drašković refers to the Ustasha concentration camps, where Serbs and others were imprisoned, as "Serbian" instead of Croatian or German or, even better, fascist or Nazi, camps. He names them, that is, according to their victims rather than, as is usual, according to their commanders. This is in keeping with the wide-spread Serb nationalist idea of natural history as a kind of biological, genetic history, based on ethnic specificity inherited, like the zeal for vengeance, over many generations. (I thank Wolfgang Klotz for this observation.)

Theme 5. Remedies

1. Although "rape" and "genocide" are official war crimes, no definition of "genocidal rape" *as such* exists in international conventions and protocols regarding the conduct of war. On July 25, 1995, the UN tribunal indicted Bos-nian Serb leader Radovan Karadžić and the Bosnian Serb military com-mander, Gen. Ratko Mladić, of war crimes, including "persecuting, selling, killing and deporting civilians throughout Bosnia and Herzegovina; sniper attacks against civilians in Sarajevo, and taking United Nations peacekeepers hostage and using them as human shields" ("U.N. Tribunal Indicts Bosnian Serb Leader and a Commander," *New York Times*, July 26, 1995: A9).

2. Personal communication, May 1994.

3. See Rafaëlle Maison, "Quelle répression des crimes internationaux," in *Women, Culture, War* (Zagreb: Drieux, forthcoming).

4. This is true to the extent that homosexuals in the U.S. armed forces, for example, are now a reality that is officially unacknowledged, to the ever greater glory of paradox.

5. These considerations bring to mind a debate at Syracuse University over the desirability of providing round-the-clock access for students to computer centers. Such access, which cost the university a not-insignificant amount of money, was, in fact, available to students on a gender-discrimi-natory basis. Although the campus computer centers might remain open all night, it was not safe for female students to go to them at all times, precisely because of the possibility that they would be raped. I remember vividly ar-guing in a faculty meeting for a more equitable system that would recognize female students' need to live on campus free from the threat of rape. The chief of the campus police spoke eloquently about how his men would be happy to provide "special protection" in the form of an escort service when-ever a female student wanted to use the computer facilities at night. He, after

all, understood such problems, as he was the father of daughters and would want them to feel protected, just as the female students should. He could not understand my objections to having the human (and civil and student) rights of women students be reduced to dependency on a generous paternalism. He was speaking from a chivalric point of view; I, from a gender-aware human rights one.

6. Marcheggiano's analysis of the ancient and medieval practices that develop into modern regulation emphasizes the influence of certain aspects of Christianity on the conduct of war. This valuable analysis should now be amplified from a gender perspective.

7. See Veuthey, *Guérilla et droit humanitaire*, note 114, for an extensive bibliography re: biological warfare.

8. I do not mean to imply that their birth mothers should necessarily take on the task of raising these children themselves. The relevant difficulties should be evident from my discussion in theme 3, "Facts."

Theme 6. Implications

1. See Beverly Allen and Mary Russo, eds., *Designing Italy: "Italy" in Europe, Africa, Asia, and the Americas* (Minneapolis: University of Minnesota Press, forthcoming), for examples of such analyses. See also George L. Mosse, *Nationalism and Sexuality* (New York: Howard Fertig, 1985), and Andrew Parker et al., *Nationalisms and Sexualities* (London: Routledge, 1993).

2. Given such reasoning, the kind of multiculturalism that prevailed in Yugoslavia prior to the mid-1980s suddenly takes on a possible new value—as a hedge against destruction by genetic weapons.

3. Footnote 5 refers the reader to "the 1972 Convention on the Prohibition of the Development, Production and Stockpiling of Bacteriological (Biological) and Toxin Weapons and on Their Destruction (the BWC)," the text of which is reproduced in Jozef Goldblat (Stockholm International Peace Research Institute [SIPRI]), *Arms Control: A Survey and Appraisal of Multilateral Agreements* (London: Taylor and Francis, 1982), 193-95.

WORKS CONSULTED

Accademia Serba delle Scienze e delle Arti. "Memorandum." Trans. Salva-tore Arcella. *Limes: Rivista italiana di geopolitica* ("La guerra in Europa: Adriatico, Jugoslavia, Balcani"). Nos. 1-2 (January-May 1993): 233-45.

Allen, Beverly, and Mary Russo, eds. *Designing Italy: "Italy" in Europe, Africa, Asia, and the Americas.* Minneapolis: University of Minnesota Press, forthcoming.

Anderson, Benedict. *Imagined Communities: Reflections on the Origin and Spread of Nationalism.* London, New York: Verso, 1993.

Bartfai, Tamas, S. J. Lundin, and Bo Rybeck. "Benefits and Threats of Developments in Biotechnology and Genetic Engineering." In SIPRI (Stockholm International Peace Research Institute) Yearbook, 1993: *World Armaments and Disarmament.* 293-305.

Bassiouni, Cherif, and committee. *United Nations Commission of Experts Report on Grave Breaches of the Geneva Conventions and Other Violations of International Humanitarian Law Committed in the Territory of the Former Yugoslavia.* New York: United Nations, May 24, 1994.

Bell-Fialkoff, Andrew. "A Brief History of Ethnic Cleansing." *Foreign Affairs* (summer 1993): 110-21.

Benjamin, Walter. *Angelus novus.* Turin: Einaudi, 1962.

_____. "Theses on the Philosophy of History." In *Illuminations,* ed. and intro. Hannah Arendt. New York: Schocken Books, 1969. 253-64.

Bocchi, Gianluca, and Mauro Ceruti. *Solidarietà o barbarie: l'Europa delle diversità contro la pulizia etnica.* Milan: Raffaello Cortina Editore, 1994.

Brownmiller, Susan, "Making Female Bodies the Battlefield." *Newsweek*, January 4, 1993: 37.

Cohen, Philip. *Desecrating the Holocaust: Serbia's Exploitation of the Holocaust as Propaganda.* Typescript, 1994. Excerpted as "Holocaust History Misappropriated," *Midstream*, vol. 38, no. 8 (November 1992): 18-20.

Colic, Velibor. *Les Bosniaques: hommes, villes, barbelés.* Paris: Galilée/Carrefour des littératures, 1993.

Cook, Stanley, Frank E. Adcock, and Martin P. Charlesworth, eds. *The Cambridge Ancient History.* Vol. 7: *The Hellenistic Monarchies and the Rise of Rome.* Cambridge: Cambridge University Press, 1975.

Council for the Defence of Human Rights and Freedoms in Prishtina. "Violation of Human and National Rights of the Albanians in Kosovo by Serbian Regime Has Features of Genocide." Presented at the World Conference on Human Rights, Vienna, June 14-25, 1993. Council for the Defence of Human Rights and Freedoms in Prishtina, Xhavit Mitrovica 15, 38000 Prishtina-Kosovo.

De Filippis, Maria. "Pochi uomini aggressivi tengono in scacco il mondo. Noi donne dobbiamo impedirlo." *noidonne* (June 1993): 94.

De la Pradelle, Paul. "Notions et sources du droit humanitaire applicable aux conflits armés." Séminaire sur l'enseignement du droit humanitaire dans les institutions militaires/Seminar on the Teaching of Humanitarian Law in Military Institutions. San Remo: International Institute of Humanitarian Law. In *Revue de droit pénal militaire et droit de la guerre* 12:2 (1973): 15-26.

Dialogue. Vol. 1, nos. 2-3. Paris (September 1992).

Dizdarević, Zlatko. *Giornale di guerra: Cronaca di Sarajevo assediata.* Palermo: Sellerio Editore, 1994.

Djilas, Aleksa. "A Profile of Slobodan Milošević." *Foreign Affairs* (summer 1993): 81-96.

Doni, Elena, and Chiara Valentini. *L'arma dello stupro: voci di donne della Bosnia.* Palermo: La Luna, 1993.

Drakulić, Slavenka. *The Balkan Express: Fragments from the Other Side of the War.* New York: HarperPerennial, 1993.

———. "Women Hide behind a Wall of Silence." *Nation* (March 1, 1993): 268, 270-72.

Draskovitch, Vuk. *Le Couteau.* Trans., from Serbian, Irina Danil; ed. Elie Robert Nicoud. Paris: J. C. Lattès, 1993.

Encyclopedia of the Holocaust. New York: Macmillan, 1990.

Enloe, Cynthia. *Bananas, Beaches & Bases: Making Feminist Sense of International Politics.* Berkeley and Los Angeles: University of California Press, 1990.

Farer, Tom J. "Illicit Means for the Conduct of Armed Conflicts." Séminaire sur l'enseignement du droit humanitaire dans les institutions militaires/ Seminar on the Teaching of Humanitarian Law in Military Institutions. San Remo: International Institute of Humanitarian Law. In *Revue de droit pénal militaire et droit de la guerre* 12:2 (1973): 153-71.

Feldman, Lada Čale, Ines Prica, and Reana Senjković, eds. *Fear, Death and Resistance: An Ethnography of War: Croatia 1991-1992.* Zagreb: Institute of Ethnology and Folklore Research, Matrix Croatica X-Press, 1993.

Finkielkraut, Alain. *Comment peut-on être croate?* Paris: Éditions Gallimard, 1992.

Folnegović-Smalc, Vera. "Psychiatric Aspects of the Rapes in the War against the Republics of Croatia and Bosnia-Herzegovina." In Alexandra Stiglmayer, ed., *Mass Rape: The War against Women in Bosnia-Herzegovina.* Lincoln and London: University of Nebraska Press, 1994. 174-79.

Garde, Paul. *Vie et mort de la Yougoslavie.* Paris: Fayard, 1992.

Goldblat, Josef (Stockholm International Peace Research Institute [SIPRI]). *Arms Control: A Survey and Appraisal of Multilateral Agreements.* London: Taylor and Francis, 1982.

Gutman, Roy. *A Witness to Genocide.* New York: Macmillan, 1993.

Harvey, Sir Paul, ed. *The Oxford Companion to Classical Literature.* Oxford: Oxford University Press, 1974.

Hobsbawm, Eric. *Nations and Nationalism since 1780: Programme, Myth, Reality.* Cambridge: Cambridge University Press, 1990.

Irigaray, Luce. *Speculum of the Other Woman.* Ithaca, N.Y.: Cornell University Press, 1985.

——. *This Sex Which Is Not One.* Ithaca, N.Y.: Cornell University Press, 1985.

Janigro, Nicole. *L'esplosione delle nazioni: il caso jugoslavo.* Milan: Feltrinelli, 1993.

Kostovic, Ivica, and Miloš Judaš, eds. *Mass Killing and Genocide in Croatia 1991/92: A Book of Evidence (Based upon the Evidence of the Division of Information, the Ministry of Health of the Republic of Croatia).* Zagreb: Hrvatska Sveučilišna Naklada, 1992.

Lonzi, Carla. "We Spit on Hegel." In Paola Bono and Sandra Kemp, eds., *Italian Feminist Thought: A Reader.* Oxford: Blackwell, 1991. 40-59. Translated from Carla Lonzi, *Sputiamo su Hegel—La donna clitoridea e la donna vaginale, e altri scritti.* Milan: Scritti di Rivolta Femminile, 1974.

MacKinnon, Catharine. "Crimes of War, Crimes of Peace." In Stephen Shute, and Susan Hurley, eds., *On Human Rights: The Oxford Amnesty Lectures, 1993.* New York: Basic Books, 1993. 83-109.

_____. "Turning Rape into Pornography: Postmodern Genocide." *Ms.,* vol. 4, no. 1 (July-August 1993): 24-30.

Magas, Branka. *The Destruction of Yugoslavia: Tracking the Break-up 1990-92.* London and New York: Verso, 1993.

Marcheggiano, Arturo. *Diritto umanitario e sua introduzione nella regolamentazione dell'esertico italiano.* Vol. 1. Rome: Stato maggiore dell'esercito, 1994.

Maresca, Adolfo. "La notion générale et les sources du droit humanitaire." Séminaire sur l'enseignement du droit humanitaire dans les institutions militaires/Seminar on the Teaching of Humanitarian Law in Military Institutions. San Remo: International Institute of Humanitarian Law. In *Revue de droit pénal militaire et droit de la guerre* 12:2 (1973): 28-45.

Meron, Theodor. "The Case for War Crimes Trials in Yugoslavia." *Foreign Affairs* (summer 1993): 122-35.

_____. "Common Rights of Mankind in Gentili, Grotius and Suárez." *American Journal of International Law,* vol. 85, no. 1 (January 1991): 110-16.

Morgan, Robin. *The Demon Lover: On the Sexuality of Terrorism.* New York: W. W. Norton, 1990.

Nahoum-Grappe, Véronique. "L'épuration ethnique: désastre et stupeur." In Véronique Nahoum-Grappe, ed., *Vukovar, Sarajevo . . . : la guerre en ex-Yougoslavie.* Paris: Éditions Esprit, 1993. 45-79.

NATO (?). *Biological Warfare Defense.* Supplied by the Italian Society for International Organizations, Rome. Further documentary information not available.

NATO *Handbook on the Medical Aspects of* NBC *Defensive Operations. Part II—Biological.* AMedP-6. August 31, 1973.

Parker, Andrew, et al. *Nationalisms and Sexualities.* London: Routledge, 1993.

"Pašić, Ehlimana." *Violentate: lo stupro-etnico in Bosnia-Erzegovina.* Rome: Armando Editore, 1993.

Petrović, Drazen, and Luigi Condorelli. "L'ONU et la crise Yougoslave." In *Annuaire français de droit international,* vol. 38 Éditions du CNRS, Paris (1992): 32-60.

Pfaff, William. "Invitation to War." *Foreign Affairs* (summer 1993): 97-109.

Pirjevec, Joze. *Il giorno di San Vito: Jugoslavia 1918-1992, Storia di una trage-dia.* Turin: Nuova ERI, 1993.

Rieff, David. *Slaughterhouse: Bosnia and the Failure of the West.* New York: Simon & Schuster, 1995.

Riva, Gigi, and Marco Ventura. *Jugoslavia: il nuovo medioevo.* Milan: Mursia, 1992.

Roberts, Adam, and Richard Guelff, eds. *Documents on the Laws of War.* 2d ed. Oxford: Oxford University Press, 1989.

Robertson, David. *A Dictionary of Modern Defence and Strategy.* London: Europa Publications, 1987.

Roux, Michel. "Tre testi per capire una tragedia." *Limes: Rivista italiana di geopolitica* ("La guerra in Europa: Adriatico, Jugoslavia, Balcani"). Nos. 1-2 (January-May 1993): 229-32.

Salvoldi, Valentino, and Lush Gjergji. *Resistenza nonviolenta nella ex-Jugoslavia: Dal Kossovo, la testimonianza dei protagonisti.* Bologna: Editrice missionaria italiana, 1993.

Seifert, Ruth. "War and Rape: A Preliminary Analysis." In Alexandra Stiglmayer, ed., *Mass Rape: The War against Women in Bosnia-Herzegovina.* Lincoln and London: University of Nebraska Press, 1994. 54-72.

Senjković, Reana. "In the Beginning There Were a Coat of Arms, a Flag, and a 'Pleter.' " In Feldman, Prica, and Senjković, eds., 24-51.

Stato Maggiore dell'Esercito, Ispettorato dell'Arma di Artiglieria e per la Difesa NBC, Ufficio NBC. *Aggressivi biologici,* no. 6295 (1983).

Stiglmayer, Alexandra, ed. *Mass Rape: The War against Women in Bosnia-Herzegovina.* Lincoln and London: University of Nebraska Press, 1994.

Stock, Thomas. "Chemical and Biological Weapons: Developments and Proliferation." SIPRI (Stockholm International Peace Research Institute) Yearbook 1993: *World Armaments and Disarmament.* 259-91.

United Nations. *Charter of the United Nations and Statute of the International Court of Justice.* New York: United Nations, n.d.

United Nations Commission of Experts Report on Grave Breaches of the Geneva Conventions and Other Violations of International Humanitarian Law Committed in the Territory of the Former Yugoslavia. See Bassiouni.

United Nations Economic and Social Council. "Rape and Abuse of Women in the Territory of the Former Yugoslavia." Document E/CN.4/1994/5, June 30, 1993.

United Nations General Assembly. "Armes chimiques et bactériologiques (biologiques)." General Document A/48/100, June 15, 1993, section 62: 135-44.

──────. "Chemical and Bacteriological (Biological) Weapons: Report of the First Committee." General Document A/48/666, December 7, 1993. Rapporteur: Macaire Kabore.

──────. "Convention on the Prohibition of the Development, Production and Stockpiling of Bacteriological (Biological) and Toxin Weapons and on Their Destruction." Document A/RES/2826 (26), February 25, 1972.

──────. "Final Report of the Commission of Experts Established Pursuant to Security Council Resolution 780 (1992)." Chair, Commission of Experts, Cherif Bassiouni. General Document S/1994/674, May 27, 1994.

──────. "Question of General and Complete Disarmament: Report of the Secretary-General on Chemical and Bacteriological (Biological) Weapons and the Effects of Their Possible Use." Prepared by Group of Consultant Experts on Chemical and Bacteriological (Biological) Weapons, William Epstein, Chairman. General Document A/7575, July 1, 1969.

United Nations General Assembly Security Council. "The Situation of Human Rights in the Territory of the Former Yugoslavia." Document A/48/92, S/25341, February 26, 1993.

Verri, Generale C. A. I protocolli aggiuntivi alle convenzioni di Ginevra del 12 agosto 1949. Rome: Rassegna della Giustizia Militare, extract of nos. 4-5, 1978.

Veuthey, Michel. "Comportement et statut des combattants." Séminaire sur l'enseignement du droit humanitaire dans les institutions militaires/Seminar on the Teaching of Humanitarian Law in Military Institutions. San Remo: International Institute of Humanitarian Law. In Revue de droit pénal militaire et droit de la guerre 12:2 (1973): 47-56.

──────. Guérilla et droit humanitaire. Geneva: International Committee of the Red Cross, 1983.

VV. AA. La guerra in Europa: Adriatico, Jugoslavia, Balcani. Limes: Rivista italiana di geopolitica, nos. 1-2 (January-May 1993).

Weinberg, Bill, and Dorie Wilsnack. "War at the Crossroads: An Historical Guide through the Balkan Labyrinth." Pamphlet. New York: Balkan War Resource Group, 1993.

Weller, Marc. "The International Response to the Dissolution of the Socialist Federal Republic of Yugoslavia." American Journal of International Law, vol. 86 (1992): 569-607.

Wheeler, Roxann. " 'My Savage,' 'My Man': Color, Gender and Nation in Eighteenth-Century British Narrative." Ph.D. diss., Syracuse University, 1994.

Woodward, Susan L. *Balkan Tragedy: Chaos and Dissolution after the Cold War.* Washington, D.C.: Brookings Institution, 1995.

Zaccaria, Giuseppe. *Noi, criminali di guerra: storie vere dalla ex-Jugoslavia.* Milan: Baldini and Castoldi, 1994.

Zanzotto, Andrea. *Il galateo in bosco.* Milan: Mondadori, 1978.

APPENDIX

For Contributions

Addresses and telephone and fax numbers of Zagreb
groups helping survivors, numbers of bank accounts
(personal checks and money orders in U.S. dollars accepted)

Bedem Ljubavi
Vlaska 70A
41000 Zagreb, Croatia
tel: (385) (1) 451-056; fax: (385) (1) 451-861)
Make checks payable to "Bedem Ljubavi" and send to
Account # 72600-3-100-03061-5
Croatia Bank
Gajeva 2
41000 Zagreb, Croatia

Bišer
Bosanska 1
41000 Zagreb, Croatia
tel/fax: (385) (1) 570-519
Make checks payable to "Bišer."

Kareta
Vlaska 70 A
41000 Zagreb, Croatia
tel/fax: (385) (1) 414-834
Make checks payable to "Kareta."

Žena BiH
Gotovceva 8
41000 Zagreb, Croatia
tel/fax: (385) (1) 530-481
Make checks payable to "Žena BiH" and send to
Account # 243 520 9673
Zagrebacka Banka
01 21 24 Nama Remiza
Ozaljska 2
Zagreb, Croatia

To Contribute to the Work of the Tribunal

Write to the Registrar at the following address, informing him/
her of your intention to contribute:

The Registrar
International Criminal Tribunal for the former Yugoslavia
P.O. Box 13888
2501 EW The Hague
The Netherlands
The Registrar will reply with an address to which you may
send a donation. This procedure meets UN regulations.
Checks should be made out to "The Registrar of the I.C.T.Y."

To Contribute to the Fund for Families of
Journalists Killed in the War

Make check or money order payable to "Foundation for Support of Families of Croatian Journalists Killed or Wounded in The Defensive War" and send to
Account # 30101-620-16-2421732736
Zagrebacka Banka
01 21 24 Nama Remiza
Ozaljska 2
Zagreb, Croatia

To Contribute to the "No Peace Without Justice"
Committee of Parliamentarians, Mayors, and Citizens for
New International Justice Campaign to Establish a
Permanent War Crimes Tribunal

No Peace Without Justice
866 United Nations Plaza, #4014
New York, NY 10017
Make checks payable to "Transnational Radical Party: No Peace Without Justice."

INDEX

Compiled by Laurie Reith Winship

BEVERLY ALLEN is associate professor of French, Italian, comparative literature, and women's studies at Syracuse University, where she directs the Humanities Doctoral Program. She is the author of *Andrea Zanzotto: The Language of Beauty's Apprentice* (1988); the editor of *Pier Paolo Pasolini: The Poetics of Heresy* (1982) and *The Defiant Muse: Italian Feminist Poems from the Middle Ages to the Present* (1986); and the coeditor (with Mary Russo) of *Designing Italy: "Italy" in Europe, Africa, Asia, and the Americas* (forthcoming, Minnesota).